"This is fascinating stuff. And I am sure I would have followed in a similarly circuitous path had I not happened upon some rather incriminating photos of NBC executives at a network junket in 1979."

· **Bob Costas**, *Hall of Fame broadcaster*

"I know the hard work it takes to be the best on the field and this book makes you appreciate what it takes to be the best in the broadcast studio. A fun and enlightening look at the careers of some of the all-time greats."

· **Jerry Rice**, *Hall of Fame wide receiver*

"This is a great read for all sports fans. Sharp, witty, and insightful, Scott Reiss has compiled REAL stories from many of our favorite media personalities."

· **Andrew Luck**, *Pro Bowl quarterback*

"Learning the hard work and sacrifices the voices of my 'sports life' have gone through makes me love and respect them all so much more. Great read."

· **Darius Rucker**, *Multi-Platinum singer & songwriter*

"As an athlete I was on the other side of their experiences, answering their questions and giving them something to talk about. But reading their stories taught me they had the same determination, tenacity, endurance & belief in themselves as the athletes they report on. A fun and insightful read from a different perspective in the sports world."

· **Kristi Yamaguchi**, *Olympic gold medalist, author*

"The rise to the top is never a straight path, but one thing it always is, at least in the world of sports broadcasting, is hilarious. *Where They Were Then* brilliantly memorializes some of these impossible-to-believe stories from those who turned into the biggest names… in their own words."

· **Darren Rovell**, *Sports Business Writer, ESPN, CNBC, The Action Network*

"Entertaining stories about life in small media markets. Must-read for sports fans and for those who aspire to a career in television."

· **Kenny Albert**, *Play-by-play announcer, FOX Sports, TNT, MSG*

"*Where They Were Then* is an inspiring and informative book written by first-rate sports broadcasters who share with us their career journeys, from apprenticeship to professional. Regardless of your current line of work, this is a must-read for those who appreciate the value of working toward mastery of craft."

· **Steve Lavin**, *Former head basketball coach, UCLA & St. John's University; analyst, FOX Sports, CBS Sports*

"Some are born great, some achieve greatness, and some have greatness thrust upon them. But as these stories will show you, most sportscasters obtain it by knocking loudly on as many doors as they can find, behind one of which greatness is loitering slothfully, waiting to be impressed by persistence or pestering. Or both: I mean just read what my man Kenny Mayne had to do!"

· **Keith Olbermann**, *Award-winning sports & news anchor*

"Oftentimes we forget about the years of backstory that brought our heroes to where they are presently. Or at least we glamorize the rough road to greatness that they've traveled, casting a dark shadow on our own setbacks. This book uses transparency, humility, and humor to not only shed light on what it takes to excel, but also inspire something in the reader that we all need: perseverance."

· **Zach Filkins**, *Guitarist & founding member,*
OneRepublic

"I know how difficult it is to reach the big leagues as a ballplayer. This book offers great insight into what it takes to reach the big leagues as a broadcaster. Really entertaining read."

· **John Smoltz**, *Hall of Fame pitcher; analyst, MLB*
Network

"*Where They Were Then* is a must-read for fans of these iconic broadcasters. It's also a terrific 'how-to' manual for young people interested in broadcast and digital journalism. Their stories of grit and determination and ultimately the payoff of success… will serve as an effective blueprint... and inspiration."

· **Craig Stevens**, *News anchor, WSVN-TV (Miami);*
former instructor of communication, University of
Miami & Barry University

"These broadcasters have told so many great stories over the years, but the best ones might be their own. I enjoyed every page."

· **Shawn Estes**, *MLB All-Star pitcher; analyst, NBC*
Sports Bay Area

WHERE THEY WERE THEN

Sportscasters

ISBN: 978-1-7377178-7-4 (Paperback)
ISBN: 978-1-7377178-6-7 (eBook)

First printing edition 2021

Printed in the United States of America

Son & Reign Publishers, LLC
PO Box 181
Hinsdale, IL 60522

sonreignpublishers@gmail.com

CONTENTS

This book is dedicated to Sheldon Reiss. Thanks, Dad, for your unwavering support. And your unconditional belief—which wasn't always warranted, but was always appreciated.

"Why Are We Here?"

There really ought to be a manual for this. A version of "Broadcasting 101"—but not the version offered in colleges and universities across the country. Rather, a real-life rundown of what it takes to break into sports television, and ultimately rise to the top of one of the most competitive businesses imaginable.

Every contributor to this book is an unmitigated success story. We reached the pinnacle of our profession. Whether that means ESPN, MLB Network, NBC Sports, or any combination of national network powerhouses, this is all "dream job" kind of stuff.

To be clear, this is not about the dream. Forgive the cliché—it's about the journey, not the destination. A journey that is unique to each of us, yet relatable to all of us. A journey so surreal and surprising, so frustrating and funny, so ridiculous and rewarding, it simply deserves to be told.

My personal tales of small-market television absurdity have played to rave reviews in social gatherings for almost two decades. Bar room banter at its finest. But even in their most organized, articulate splendor, my stories would fill a pamphlet, not a book. Which is why they have remained "off the record" for so long.

How did I finally get to this point? A few years back, I was eating dinner with a friend who was, at the time, smack dab in the middle of the arduous process of trying to break into the "business." You might say, the quintessential target audience. I had her in hysterics, spewing ludicrous tales of my former job as a news/sports anchor in Utica, New York. At one point, she said matter-of-factly, "You really should write a book."

"Funny you should mention that," I responded. "I've wanted to do that for years." And I offered up my "pamphlet" excuse.

And then...boom! (Or as we in the broadcasting world like to say, "Boom goes the dynamite!")

"What about your TV friends? Don't they have similar stories?"

There it was. Genius in its simplicity. Strength in numbers. The idea rocked me like a backward-running TelePrompTer (which has happened, by the way). We all have stories that would be invaluable to the aspiring sportscaster, but—more to the point—entertaining to millions (dare to dream, right?) of sports junkies. Hey, it's TV. It's sports. It's mainstream.

What follows are the accounts of friends and former colleagues. Some names you will likely recognize, others perhaps not. All are incredibly talented; yet had they not navigated a series of trials and tribulations during their formative years, that talent would not be on display for the world to see.

Which national sportscaster once did the nightly news with an IV in his arm? Which one helped usher in Shaquille O'Neal's rap career? Which one helped expose an illegal prostitution ring? Not only will you find those answers in these pages, you'll read it right from the source—in the first-person narrative of some of your favorite TV personalities. I considered doing the "normal" biographical book thing—conducting interviews, taking notes, telling other people's stories—but ultimately decided that the essence of this group's greatness is its distinct, recognizable writing styles. Nobody can tell Kenny Mayne's story better than Kenny Mayne. So why would I dare try?

And for the thousands of aspiring anchors and reporters toiling away (or hoping to toil away) in every nook and cranny of the nation, these accounts will transcend celebrity and invoke reality.

You want to be a sportscaster? Let this serve as the ever-elusive manual, a literary roadmap to the landmines of the business. The rest of you, simply embrace the experience and appreciate the long and winding road to the top of the professional mountain.

"The Guy Who Introduces *Star Trek*"

Scott Reiss

·WPGX, Panama City, FL   ·Comcast SportsNet Bay Area
·WUTR, Utica, NY   ·KTVU, Oakland, CA
·KCOY, Santa Maria, CA   ·Stanford Football/Basketball
·ESPN

Chris Berman is the poster child for ESPN fame, having worked at the network since shortly after its inception in 1979. I was fortunate enough to get to know "Boomer" a bit during my eight years in Bristol, and have seen him on occasion since. He is a fantastic talent and a genuinely good guy who deserves all the accolades and admiration that have come his way. But Chris will be the first to tell you, he got lucky. He signed on with a fledgling national network that wound up an international phenomenon. He got a cool job in his early 20s that allowed him to flourish both professionally and financially, and there was never much reason to go anywhere else.

Most of us navigated a decidedly different path to glory. We did "time" in small towns, changing jobs every couple of years, working terrible hours for terrible (or no) money, lugging heavy camera equipment from event to event, shooting our stuff, editing our stuff, producing our stuff, all for the privilege of delivering high school volleyball highlights and post-rodeo reaction during the final three minutes of a nightly middle-of-nowhere newscast. Sounds dreamy, I know. Oh, and did I mention those jobs were almost impossible to get?

My professional quest began in the spring of 1994. I graduated from Stanford with a bachelor's degree in communication and a master's degree in sociology. While most of my friends were moving on to medical school or well-paying jobs in finance or business consulting, I moved back home to Los Angeles to pursue my passion.

A year later, I had applied to what seemed like every small-market TV station in America (though I did draw the line at the "booming tropical paradise of Guam," a staple of the Broadcasting & Cable magazine classifieds). Week after week, the rejection letters piled up. I still have about 30 of them.

The result? Radio (or TV) silence, with rare exception. One of those exceptions was WABG-TV in Greenville, Mississippi, the self-proclaimed "Heart and Soul of the Delta." The station had an opening for a sports anchor/reporter and invited me in for an interview.

I'll never forget driving my rental car out of the Little Rock airport on the eve of that big interview, heading south on I-530. I had never been to the South (Mardi Gras hardly counts), and it felt like a different world. A big city kid, all alone on the highway, flat open space in every direction, as far as the eye could see. Truly surreal.

I had booked a room in Pine Bluff, Arkansas, which sits midway between Little Rock and Greenville. It was almost midnight when I pulled into the Days Inn parking lot, eager, exhausted, and anxious in equal parts. Once inside, I approached the front desk, where a 350-pound man with a massive, scraggly beard and bright red suspenders was too engrossed in late-night television to acknowledge my existence.

"Excuse me," I said. "I think I have a reservation."

After a lengthy pause, he glanced up at me and responded with his Billy Bob Thornton "*Sling Blade*"-esque pipes.

"You *think* you have a reservation?"

6

Heart in throat.

"Well, I'm pretty sure I have a reservation."

I gave him my name, and he sifted through his box of index cards.

"Oh, here it is."

Feeling reassured, I asked, "Do you give a discount for AAA members?"

This time more a glare than a glance.

"Sometimes."

I pressed my luck.

"Well, would this be one of those times?"

And the inevitable.

"Nope."

Against my better judgment, I pressed my luck further.

"Why would that be?"

"Because it's UAPB homecoming weekend."

As I did the mental math...U-A-P-B...University of Arkansas at Pine Bluff...he continued, this time unprompted.

"But I could tell you ain't with them, 'cause you much too pale."

Please don't shoot me.

"Yep," he was now on a roll, "Those of 'em who know how to read will probably even be here on time!"

And with that, I took my room key, prayed for a deadbolt on the door and retreated to find my room. Welcome to the South, you sheltered California kid.

The next morning, I drove the remaining two hours to WABG in Greenville, the local ABC affiliate. First impression of the station—bars on every window. Very comforting.

The interview was pleasant, albeit brief. A tour, a nice conversation, some background about what they cover—Delta State and Mississippi Valley State football being the headliners, the latter of which is the alma mater of Jerry Rice. Not surprisingly, they're pretty proud of that. I did not do an on-set audition.

I remember the news director asking me if I could shoot my own video. The correct answer was, of course, "yes," regardless of whether it was actually true. You want a job like that, you tell them what they need to hear and figure it out later. But I was naïve and honest and said something to the effect of, "Not really, but I am more than willing to learn." Needless to say, I didn't get the gig.

The longer my unemployment dragged on, the more desperate I became. To my credit (and my parents' as well, since it was their dime), I got majorly—some would argue insanely—proactive. I pinpointed the area of the country with the most small and medium markets within reasonable driving distance of one another. As coincidence would have it, that triangulation took me back to the South: northern Florida, southern Georgia, and Alabama. I sent tapes to every affiliate in Tallahassee, Gainesville, Panama City, Macon, Augusta, Albany, and Dothan. Then came the follow-up phone calls, telling every news director I could reach that I was "going to be in the area" and wanted to stop by and chat, if they could spare 15 minutes. Open jobs, no open jobs, news, sports, didn't matter. I needed to force the issue. Surely somebody would be impressed enough by the effort to give me a shot.

Two weeks later, I flew into Atlanta, rented a car, and made the rounds. Five days, 11 interviews, plenty of good will, a ton of fried food…and no job offers. The only promising lead was a Fox startup in Panama City, FL, with a news director who seemed impressed by my ambition and somewhat confident in my potential. It just so happened he had a news anchor/reporter position coming open in a couple of months, and he'd keep me in mind.

That was February, 1995. In mid-May, he called me and expressed regret that while he would liked to have hired me, the outgoing anchor was a female, and he therefore needed a female to replace her (why he couldn't have done that math three months prior remains a mystery to this day). I remember hanging up the phone on the verge of tears, for the first time sincerely believing I would never get a chance in this awful business.

Then I got a crazy idea. Why not put this guy to the test? He says he wants to hire me but can't, due to circumstances. Let's see if that's really true or just a line. After a heart-to-heart with Mom and Dad (who were willing to do just about anything at that point to ease my pain and/or get me out of the house), I called back Andy Shore at WPGX-TV in Panama City. I asked him if I could move out there and work for free, just to get the experience and better my resume tape. He wasn't expecting such a proposition.

"Um, the problem is, there are laws against that sort of thing. I can't put you to work and not pay you, unless it's an internship."

And there was my opening.

I'll spare you the back and forth and merely report that three weeks later I was driving from Los Angeles to the Florida panhandle to begin my TV career. Before my first day of "work,"

I stopped by Gulf Coast Community College to register for one unit of internship credit. My Stanford master's degree did not get me a break on the $104 tuition.

Andy Shore gave me no guarantees of anything other than on-the-job experience in a TV newsroom. As I would soon find out, "newsroom" was somewhat of a loose term. But on Friday of my first week—July 4th, 1995—I wrote and reported my first on-air feature package. A wrap-up of the Panama City Independence Day parade, featuring headline performer Lynyrd Skynyrd. I'm sure you remember the concert.

On some level, WPGX was the perfect first gig, because the "newsroom" was more like a cubicle. The entire on-air staff consisted of three people, which meant I was 4th on the totem pole right from the jump. The "newscasts" at 6:00 p.m. and 9:00 p.m. were all of five minutes in duration, with the 6:00 version leading into *Star Trek* at 6:05. The anchor would end each night's news by saying, "Thanks for watching. *Star Trek* is next."

No joke, when people around town recognized him on the street, they would exclaim, "Hey, it's the guy who introduces *Star Trek*!" You can't put a price on that level of fame.

My indoctrination into "hard news" came less than two weeks into my Panama City tenure. I happened to be in the newsroom after everyone else had gone, and I heard the scanner blowing up with police chatter about a murder in town. It awoke my inner newshound, so much so that I (the unpaid intern) drove a stick-shift news vehicle that I was neither authorized nor qualified to drive, shot video on a camera that I was neither authorized nor qualified to shoot, and covered the story.

Over the next five months, I evolved into a *bona fide* (albeit still unpaid) news reporter. I turned stories, filled in introducing *Star Trek* on the anchor desk, and was even allowed to "enterprise" a few sports specials, primarily because they had so much dead air on this network they'd put pretty much anything on. All the while, maintaining a 4.0 GPA at Gulf Coast Community College.

At summer's end, I assembled a resume tape that got me my first "real" job offer—weekday news reporter/weekend news anchor at WUTR, the ABC affiliate in Utica, NY. Honestly, I wasn't sure exactly where Utica was. And honestly, I didn't care. The job paid $13,500 a year (plus overtime!), which was significantly more than zero.

I learned quickly at WUTR that anchoring the news entails more than just reading copy. In this particular case, *a lot* more. You might have noticed that little earpiece contraption that anchors wear while delivering the news? It's known as an IFB (short for "Interruptible foldback," which is not relevant—I actually had to look it up), and it allows people in the control room to speak directly to the anchors when necessary. Sadly, it was the "when necessary" part that escaped the fine technical staff of WUTR.

Our IFB system was…flawed. It did not allow for specific, person-to-person conversation between control room and news desk. Instead of, say, the producer giving instructions exclusively to the anchor, we had what was essentially an open broadcast channel. A free-for-all. So when anybody on headset spoke, everybody with an earpiece heard. Producer, director, assistant director, technical director, master control operator, tape operator—when any of them said anything to anyone, the anchors heard it. *While attempting to deliver the news.* Now you'd think, given the delicate context of a live newscast, there would be some sort of protocol in place to discourage folks from saying any more than was absolutely necessary at any given time. Or at the very least, that common sense and/or common courtesy would prevail. Sadly, none of that was the case. I can't tell you how many times I was reading a "hard news" story while simultaneously hearing random people work out the specifics of their impending dinner plans. Silver lining…it made me quite proficient at blocking out distractions while executing live TV. So there's that.

Another charming nuance of small-market TV (although disturbingly, some large-market stations are beginning to use it for cost-cutting reasons): the anchor-controlled TelePrompter.

As if the degree of difficulty of delivering the news while Joe the technical director was telling Dave the tape guy a dirty joke in your ear wasn't high enough, we had to do so while controlling our own prompter. You know, the gadget that allows anchors to read text while looking straight into the camera? Ideally, somebody controls the script as it scrolls through. At WUTR, the anchors did it themselves, using either a knob behind the desk or a foot pedal. Either way, it was an acquired skill.

And even if you successfully navigated the prompter rolling and the control room yapping, there was the alarmingly consistent threat of "operator error" during a newscast. Not surprising, I guess. Just as this was an entry-level job for the anchors, it was an entry-level job for folks behind the scenes. And that made for some interesting TV moments.

During one newscast, we were "teasing" a story coming up after commercial. The anchor read her copy, "Just ahead, our weekly 'Kidz Corner' segment!" complete with crayon-like graphics at the bottom of the screen that read "Kidz Corner." All good, except that the tape operator rolled the wrong tape, so instead of seeing kids frolicking in school, we saw death and destruction in the form of a fiery train crash.

Even better was the time I was delivering a story on municipal housing. I appeared on camera and read my copy—something to the effect: "Local officials using city funds for the good of the community," only to have them roll video of a man shooting up heroin. Turns out, our municipal housing file video was on a tape adjacent to our drug file video. Somebody cued the tape incorrectly. Whoops.

While the on-air blunders were laughable, the off-air environment was anything but. And this was the root of my disdain for WUTR. There was a toxic "us versus them" struggle between those of us who saw this as a stepping-stone to bigger and better things, and the Utica "lifers" for whom TV was a job, not a career. The former included most of the on-air talent. The latter ranged from production assistants all the way up to the general manager.

I will not identify him by name, but this general manager went to absurd—and deliberate—lengths to keep us from advancing our careers. He locked up the master copies of all newscasts. He changed the entire station routing system to make it impossible for anyone to record newscasts in the edit area. He also issued an edict that banned employees from the building outside of scheduled working hours and prohibited any "dubs" being made of newscasts (which were under lock and key anyway).

It became virtually impossible for anchors and reporters to assemble resume tapes and ultimately get other jobs. It was tantamount to "TV jail." This was not 2021, when digital editing allows us to update reels on our laptops. We were beholden to the station's antiquated equipment.

Our only workaround was a tape machine in the hallway on which we were (somehow) still able to record our own copy of a newscast. That is, until Rick decided otherwise. I honestly can't remember Rick's last name or his job title (something on the technical side). But I will never forget the tenacity he showed in attempting to ensure our eternal servitude to WUTR.

Rick's daily routine included the following: check the tape machine during every newscast to see if someone was recording it, and if so, eject the tape. Essentially, a random employee sabotaging young professionals' chances for advancement, for no apparent reason other than he felt like it.

For me, the quintessential Utica moment came on the night of the 1996 mayoral election. I had the good fortune of staking out city hall to get reaction from the eventual winner. Incredibly, the city was so depressed during that time, that the citizens re-elected a former mayor from the 1970s who was then 73-years-old and quite possibly borderline senile. Because hey, they longed for the good old days. Problem (well, one of them) was, Ed Hanna was as media-unfriendly as they came. He hated the camera, and it hated him back. So when Mayor-elect Hanna emerged from city hall following his triumph, rather than embrace his moment in the sun and proclaim his appreciation and love for the city, the 73-year-old opted to *sprint* away from me and my cameraman, dive into his brown Buick, and peel out of the parking lot. You can't make this stuff up.

It was that night I decided I simply *had* to get out. I resigned myself to leaving Utica with or without another job. In January, 1997, I packed up the car, headed back to California, and never looked back. Weeks later, I got incredibly lucky and received an offer from the CBS affiliate in Santa Maria, California. It would become my first full-time on-air sports job. Onward and way upward.

Perhaps you've heard the famous Keith Olbermann line about Bristol in the rear-view mirror. Let me assure you—as one who has seen that as well—nothing compares to Utica in the rear-view mirror. But as much as I struggled with the city and all it entailed, I will forever appreciate the experience and perspective it provided en route to a successful TV career.

"The 'Elevator Guy' from Letterman"

Photo Courtesy: WMGC

-From The Author:

Trey Wingo, in addition to having one of the coolest names in broadcasting, is also one of the coolest people. When I first arrived at ESPN in 2000, the anchors' desks were all in one massive room, divided into "pods"—oversized cubicles with four desks and four mini-walls. Trey was in my pod (along with Bob Halloran and Betsy Ross, for you serious ESPN historians). It was there, after one of my first shows, that he complimented me on my on-air style. Trey was legit, established. I was nobody. The fact that he even noticed what I was doing made me feel like I belonged. Which may or may not have been the case, but I always appreciated the verbal fist-bump (before actual fist-bumps were a thing).

Trey Wingo

·WMGC, Binghamton, NY   ·ESPN
·WFMZ, Allentown, PA   ·Pro Football Network
·KSDK, St. Louis, IL   ·Caesars Sportsbook

I remember it like it was yesterday, even though it was 32 years ago. I was sitting on a bus on my way from Binghamton, New York, to Salisbury, Maryland. It was somewhere on that solitary ride that I asked myself, "What the heck am I doing with my life?" And that, ladies and gentlemen, was about as low as you can go.

I was just a year into my first TV job in upstate NY, but ready to put together a resume tape. Problem was, the equipment at my Binghamton station was borderline-useless, so my former news director who had moved to Salisbury offered to let me work on the tape there. How bad was that first station? So bad that in 1989 there wasn't a TelePrompter; so bad that the news studio had a tin corrugated roof and every time it rained it sounded like we were doing a show in the middle of a hailstorm. You don't know how good you have it until you've lived through how bad it's been.

All my college friends were graduating from law school with cushy six-figure jobs, or really hitting their strides in their chosen careers. I was on a bus in the middle of nowhere trying to fake a 5:00 p.m. sportscast just to find my way to a job that paid me more than the $10,999 a year I got for talking about sports. Side note: they did allow me two hours of overtime every week, so my salary soared to almost $11,500. SCORE!

How did I find myself in that position? Of course, it was my fault. I went to college with all the intentions of religiously pursuing a degree in radio and television broadcasting. That lasted about…two months. When I found out every bar around campus had a happy hour, let's just say my thought process changed. So did my major, like five times. By the time I actually did graduate in four and a half years (sorry, Mom and Dad), I had no intention of working nights and weekends, grinding in Bucksnort, Tennessee. (There aren't actually any TV stations in Bucksnort, but I just really love the name of that town). No, that life was behind me. I was gonna get a cushy office job doing something else.

So instead of local TV upon graduation, I became an account executive for the public relations firm of Rogers and Cowan in its Washington, D.C., office. I had a great apartment in the Glover Park area of our nation's capital and a Monday-Friday gig with holidays and weekends off—plus I had my own office. So, what was it I actually did? It was my job to make sure that any time there was press about something a client of ours was sponsoring, the article/interview made sure to include the name of the corporate sponsor. Let me tell you something, you haven't lived until you've called *The Washington Post* to make sure their coverage of the exhibit of the great muralist Diego Rivera has the words "brought to you by The Ford Motor Company" in it. Life goals achieved.

To be honest, I was terrible at this job, and I knew it. The best part of my day was something we called "lunch." It got to the point where I would walk into the office, close the door, and just read the sports pages all day. Kids, before the internet there was this thing called a newspaper where you got all the information on what happened the night before. Magical times. This was not going to end well and we all knew it, so before I could officially get fired, I decided to quit. I moved back into my parents' basement and figured I'd start the whole thing over again. Nothing says abject failure more than having a college degree, completely flaming out of your first job, and moving back in with your folks. I was the poster child for someone in need of a Matt Foley motivational-speaker-like figure in my life.

So what do you do when you've hit rock bottom? You find a way to dig yourself into an even deeper hole. I somehow got an offer to be a page at NBC. Yes, just like Jack on the old TV show *30 Rock*. I gave guided tours of the studios, handed out tickets for shows like *Donahue* and *Saturday Night Live*, worked the elevator taking the audience up to *The David Letterman Show*, and—the cherry on top of the sundae— worked in the NBC store. What's better than selling Alf dolls and *Golden Girls* coffee mugs 24 days in a row leading up to Christmas? I almost got fired there, too, as one customer thought I was being snarky when I mentioned "the left coast" when she told me she was from California. There wasn't any implication other than when you look at a map, California is on the left and New York is on the right. I guess I must have been really good at folding those *Today Show* T-shirts because otherwise I'd have been out on my butt just in time for the holidays.

That job did have its perks, though. There were about 30-40 of us all trying to make it—somehow—in the business. Working *Saturday Night Live* was fun and you haven't lived until you've gone to the post-show SNL party. And when I worked the elevator for Letterman, I had this stupid little routine I made up, reminding visitors of all the rules, what you can and can't do inside the studio. It must have had some impact, because months later, I walked into a bar with a woman I was trying to impress and some drunk dude ran up to me and said, "I know you, you're the ELEVATOR GUY from Letterman!" I peaked in 1987.

By the way, one of my 30-40 fellow pages was a guy named Tad Brown. All he ended up doing was become CEO of The Houston Rockets, before moving on to become CEO of the Philadelphia 76ers and the New Jersey Devils. Man, I hope things work out for that guy.

After two years of that, I finally put together a demo tape that sort of looked like an actual sportscast and started sending it out to stations that were hiring. I believe my hit rate on interest was close to .000078%—the exception being WMGC, the ABC affiliate in Binghamton, NY. They offered over the phone and I accepted, sight unseen. The unseen part was probably a good thing, because if I had *seen,* hawking NBC merchandise might have looked a whole lot better by comparison. Here's where it gets weird: While I was in Binghamton, you know who was also there? Two people who became colleagues of mine at ESPN: Bill Pidto and Karl Ravech. Bill was the first to arrive, and now does great work at MSG in New York, while Karl is still at ESPN and doing well. The weatherman at my first job was a guy named Bob Maxon, who is now my local weatherman in Connecticut. So strange that all of us were in one place at the same time and continued to be connected by employer and/or geography for so many years.

Whenever Bob went on vacation, I did the weather, and when I had time off, Bob did sports. Let me just say Bob was way better at breaking down the highlights of the Chenango Forks/Chenango Valley football game than I was at explaining what that Alberta clipper was doing to the jet stream or why that low pressure system was just SITTING there in the lower Atlantic.

One of my best/worst memories from WMGC? We had a high school basketball team in Johnson City, NY, that had lost something like 27 straight games. When you're talking fast, as most of us do early in our careers, linguistics become…very challenging. As I was doing the highlights one night, Johnson City came very close to being pronounced "Johnson Sh*tty" on air. While completely appropriate and emblematic of the team's success, that would've been an end-game on-air mistake.

After two-and-a-half years in Binghamton, I finally got another job offer in Allentown, Pennsylvania. By the way, that bus ride to Maryland for a better audition tape never really helped, but I have to say Salisbury was a lovely little town from what I remember of the 26 hours I spent there.

Going from Binghamton to Allentown? I was checking off all the major stops in the Northeast. The job there had some great perks, though. I was able to do some play-by-play for Lehigh University's football and basketball games. In another weird twist, the guy I replaced as the sports director in Allentown is someone you might have heard of: Rich Lerner, who's gone on to become a mainstay at The Golf Channel. Funny how that works in this business.

I was only in Allentown nine months when I got a job offer in St. Louis, Missouri. That felt SOOO big at the time. I remember when we drove into St. Louis for the first time and I saw the building where I'd be working. You should understand, it was actually a *building*. The studio in Binghamton, as I told you, was less than desirable, and the newsroom in Allentown was a trailer attached to the rest of the station. We actually had a REAL BUILDING in St. Louis. As I said, HUGE.

I spent six years there, then 23 at ESPN, and now I'm having a blast working for myself and with Caesars Sports Book, The Pro Football Network, and doing my podcast. And to think it all started from a prompter-less studio in the twin tiers of Southern New York and Northern Pennsylvania. Not sure what I'd change, if anything, as it all seems to have worked out. Pretty fun ride, too. Now, before I go, what do I have to do to make sure you mention that the Diego Rivera mural exhibit is brought to you by The Ford Motor Company?

"The Traffic Safety Advocate"

-From The Author:

Heidi Watney has done what few of us get to do—work the "red carpet" at an All-Star game. OK, the carpet was actually purple, but that's beside the point. I met Heidi in 2014 while covering the American League Wild Card game in Kansas City. We were huddled with about 30 other reporters in a narrow tunnel waiting to be let onto the field for postgame interviews. What should have been a 15-minute sardine-can simulation turned into more than 90 minutes when the game went into extra innings. Quality bonding time, to say the least. Good thing, too, because were it not for that night, this book would likely be missing one of its more entertaining chapters.

Heidi Watney

·KMPH, Fresno, CA ·NESN
·Time Warner Cable Sportsnet ·MLB Network

I'm often asked when I knew I wanted to be a sports broadcaster. It seems many expect it was a childhood fantasy of mine, that I would spend summers interviewing my teddy bears about their accomplishments. Quite the contrary. I didn't even think about this as a career path until my senior year of college. I've always loved sports. So much so, I was disappointed when I went to my first football game as a freshman at the University of San Diego and the stadium contained fewer fans than my high school stadium on a Friday night in Fresno/Clovis. *That* is when I realized how passionate I was about sports. Fast forward a few years, and my guy friends I'd watch football with would constantly implore me to become a sideline reporter. I was a natural-born performer (communications and theatre were the focus for my degree). And having women on the sidelines of games was just becoming a thing. My girlfriend was interning at the local NBC affiliate in San Diego, and suggested I try that to see if it was a fit.

Armed with my resume touting my nanny and lifeguarding skills, I drove down to KNSD in San Diego in search of an internship. I didn't even make it through the main door when the lovely woman in human resources said they had already filled their internships for the spring semester. I was a graduating senior, and as nice and persuasive as I tried to be, she just shrugged. But guess who happened to be getting back from his lunch break at that exact moment? The main sports anchor for the station—and former NFL linebacker—Jim Lazlavic. He heard my pleas about how this was my only shot at doing a college internship and told me that if I was interested in sports, their department would take me on. Turns out, that is exactly what I was looking for. Guess I was in the right place at the right time. It's one of the many times in my life I have truly felt that God stepped in to guide my way.

That internship helped me get my first actual TV job after graduation. I was fortunate to be able to start my career in my hometown of Fresno, California. But it was not a straight shot into sports, which had been the goal. I was hired to do traffic reports on the new morning show at the FOX affiliate, KMPH. It was either that or go be the weekend sports anchor in Amarillo, Texas. Granted, I had never been to Amarillo. But the offered salary of about $17,500 seemed like it might be tough to scrape by on, even in 2003. Since the hometown offer included a better salary, I accepted that job, even though it was not in sports. I felt like I could talk my way in eventually, right?

If you've ever spent much time in the Central Valley of California, you probably know there isn't much in the way of traffic. Certainly not anything close to what you'd find in Los Angeles or San Francisco. So my reports often consisted of warning drivers of hazards like…cows in the road. Once there was even a sea lion that got loose. Apparently, it swam up an aqueduct and ended up on a rural road hundreds of miles from the coast. I think they even made a children's book about it: *Chippy the Sea Lion*.

Anyway, the station quickly realized there was not a pressing need for a traffic reporter, so they dubbed me the

"Traffic Safety Advocate." I had to do stories about safe driving. I was also 22 and a habitual speeder. So after I received a pretty hefty speeding ticket, I got suspended from work. You know, because I was the "Traffic Safety Advocate."

Mercifully for this aspiring sportscaster, the weekend sports anchor left about a year after I arrived in Fresno, so you know I went straight to the news director's office to ask for that job. What did he tell me? He didn't think the Central Valley was ready for a female sportscaster. This was 2005! For the next five or six months, I spent every weekend putting together a mock sportscast. And every Monday morning I would leave that tape on the news director's desk. Eventually, he relented and gave me the job (I'm pretty sure he just couldn't find anyone he liked better that was willing to work for the pay).

Speaking of pay, the exorbitant salaries you hear about for some of the top network talent? Not a thing in small markets. Stations know they can get talent on the cheap, and they will exploit that. On the plus side, poverty loves company. And small market wages were a significant source of bonding. Some of my best times were had at the local TGI Friday's happy hour after the 10:00 p.m. newscast. Half-off appetizers and drinks— we were there every week!

One February I went to Pebble Beach for the AT&T Celebrity Pro Am golf tournament. My cousin, PGA Tour pro Nick Watney, was playing in it and I wanted to watch him, plus I had pitched it as a story idea for our newscast. My dad, a lifelong golfer and college golf coach, advised me to "post up" at one of the par-3 holes to get some easy interviews. Those holes get backed up with players waiting on the group in front of them, so some of the golfers and celebrities might have a moment for a quick interview. Most everyone I talked to was gracious and kind to this small-market reporter from Fresno asking for a moment of their time. And then there was Bill Murray. I asked the talented comedian if he wouldn't mind looking into the camera and saying, "It's time for Kopi's 5-day forecast." Kopi Sotiropulos was the popular weatherman at the station I worked at, and he was known for having locals and celebrities "tease" his forecast. Murray wasn't having any of it. He not only did not play along, he decided to mock the request to fans in the grandstands behind the hole. Playing to the crowd, Murray made me and my request the butt of his jokes. At the time, I was pretty embarrassed. Looking back, I wish I would have dished it right back to him. Instead, I packed up my camera and was done for the day.

The Fresno sports scene largely revolves around Fresno State athletics, which go on break during the summer months. While we did have the Fresno Grizzlies (AAA affiliate of the SF Giants at the time), there wasn't a whole lot else going on. But we still had to fill our sportscasts. So I pitched a "thrill-seeking" series called *Dare Heidi*, which entailed my embarking on adventures in and around the Valley—adventures that our viewers could (theoretically) emulate. This was one of my best ideas to date. I went skydiving, flew a fighter plane in a mock dogfight, drove a NASCAR-style car in a short-track race, went cliff jumping, and was looking into hang gliding when the station attorney finally stepped in and said that, upon further review it didn't seem all that safe to send a reporter (clearly an adrenaline junkie) into these potentially dangerous situations in the name of entertainment. But boy, it was fun while it lasted.

One of the first *Dare Heidi* stories was the skydiving. Since I was doing this for TV, I didn't want to do a "simple" tandem jump. So I took an eight-hour class to learn how to jump by myself: pulling my own parachute, and flying solo to the ground. My photographer spent equal time shooting video of my preparations, and also asking if I were really going to go through with it. My parents called to try to talk me out of it. But even if I wanted to (and trust me, there was a moment or two of weakness), there was no way I was going to back out with the cameras rolling. So into the sky we went, going over the jump sequence again on the way up.

I wore a jumpsuit that had a handle on each side—one for my instructor to hold onto as we exited the plane, and one for a jump-trained cameraman. I then had to wave them off before I pulled my parachute. IT WAS AMAZING. The thrill of my life. And I was lucky enough to have it all on video. My cameraman was on the ground to record my (perfect) landing and the pure joy on my face. I got to put the entire, incredible experience into a package for our newscast, and it remains one of the coolest stories I've done for TV.

The other segments were great as well. I mean, not everyone gets to fly a fighter plane in a mock dogfight. A company out of Fullerton, California, lets you do it for around $1,000 per person. A trained pilot takes you out over the Pacific Ocean, then turns the controls over to you while teaching you how to track down and "shoot" another plane. I brought along our weekend anchor so he could be the other plane in the "dogfight" for our story. He loved it! I did too…but my body did not. I not only passed out at one point, I felt like I had been run over by a truck for the next 24 hours. The G-forces of flying in one of those planes, end over end, did a number on this girl who gets motion sickness driving to the airport.

I was fortunate to always have a photographer shoot my stories. (Since my time in Fresno, many stations have gone to the "one-man band," where reporters shoot their own video and set up their own cameras on live shots.) The lone exception was a story I volunteered to shoot. Our weekend anchor was doing a special about hiking up Half Dome in Yosemite. It's a grueling 18-mile trek, and none of our photographers felt up to the task. Being the adventurous person I am, I volunteered to learn how to operate one of our smaller cameras so I could shoot the segment for my colleague. The "mini-cams" are not as bulky and heavy as regular cameras, and the anchor actually shot some of the video himself. But he needed someone to get footage of him completing the hike and doing stand-ups, so I had my first (and to this day only) experience as a videographer.

The minicams are pretty foolproof, so shooting the video itself wasn't hard. The hike was tough, but nothing I couldn't handle. Until we got to the top. The last part of the hike is approximately 1,000 steps (or maybe 1,000,000). Literally stairs cut out of granite. Then once your thighs are quivering and you feel like puking from the exertion and altitude, you get to the dome. The dome is a granite mound, straight up. There are steel cables lining one side with a wooden plank about every 10 feet. Climbers use the steel cables to hold onto as they ascend. They can rest on the wooden planks. By now you undoubtedly understand I'm not scared of heights or adventure. Trying to climb while holding a camera does present an added challenge, but still, I wasn't fazed by that. What did throw me was trying to breathe in the rarified air. I felt like an elephant was standing on my chest.

Keep in mind, I was in my mid-20s and in pretty good shape. But this was a feeling unlike any I had experienced. We got to the top, and I just lay on the ground. I think I shot a stand-up for my co-worker, but all I remember was the painful feeling in my chest. We finished the story and hiked the nine miles back down. The next day my chest was still hurting, so I went to a doctor, and it turns out I had bronchitis. The doctor couldn't believe I had completed a hike to the top of Half Dome in that condition. Good thing I had the video proof!

At one point during my tenure in Fresno, the main female anchor went on maternity leave. She was going to be out for three months, and nearly all the ladies at the station were hoping for a chance to fill her seat. All except me, that is. I was happily covering sports. But the news director—the same one who had previously told me he didn't think the Central Valley was ready for a female sportscaster—asked me to fill in for her. To say I was surprised would be an understatement. He said he liked my delivery on camera, and thought I could still do the sportscast two days a week in addition to the news. He was my boss, so I wasn't going to say no. That upset quite a few women in the news department, two in particular who didn't like me very much after that. I certainly understand why they wanted the opportunity, but the move wasn't my idea, so they had no reason to take out their anger on me. They didn't see it that way. That was probably my first experience with "cattiness" in this business.

When the anchor returned from maternity leave, my news director told me I should consider switching from sports to being a news anchor. He said I had good rapport with my co-anchors, and would go further in this business as a female covering the news instead of sports. A few years later, super-agent Scott Boras told me the same thing. I was the Red Sox sideline reporter at the time, but he told me I had a good delivery and good voice, and I could be the "next Katie Couric" if I switched to news instead of sports, where I would always have an uphill battle to be the "lead" since I wasn't a man. I told both of them the same thing: I'm in this business because I am passionate about sports, not just to be on TV. And, quite frankly, the news is depressing. I hated talking about children getting hurt or dying, or about war and politics. That's one thing I love about sports: it's uplifting and fun (most of the time).

In the summer of 2007, the MLB All-Star Game was in San Francisco, so I asked my boss if I could cover it. To my delight, he agreed. A three-man crew—me, a cameraman, and an intern—got our credentials and headed to the Bay Area. We filed reports on every story we could possibly relate to the Central Valley. One story we really wanted to do—but had not prepared for beforehand—involved being in McCovey Cove during the Home Run Derby, where there was sure to be a bevy of baseballs making splash landings. I figured we could just rent a kayak and paddle out there. Rookie mistake! That cove was so full of kayaks and boats there wasn't an inch of water left uncovered. So I did what any intrepid reporter would do: I asked if anyone would let me jump onto his boat. There I was, climbing down from the boardwalk onto a stranger's kayak with my microphone to do a report from the middle of the "flotilla" of kayaks in the Cove. Somehow I managed to stay mostly dry, and more importantly, so did the microphone.

That experience covering MLB's crown jewel event—as well as Barry Bonds' chase for home run number 756 later that summer—laid the groundwork for my eventual career moves. See, as the hometown girl covering the Fresno and Central Valley sports scene, I was happy. I stayed at KMPH for about four-and-a-half years. But after getting a taste of professional sports and an itch to travel outside the area in which I had lived my entire life, I decided to "go for it." That winter I put together a demo reel and sent it to four different agents. One of them flew me to New York City for an in-person meeting, where he asked if he could pass my reel on to New England Sports Network (NESN). The Red Sox sideline reporter job had suddenly come open, and spring training was already underway. Naturally I said yes, though I didn't really believe a girl from Cali would be hired for that job. Again, I feel like God put me in the right place at the right time.

A week later, I was on a plane to Boston for my first round of meetings. Then NESN sent me to Los Angeles to do an on-camera audition during the Sox' exhibition game against the Dodgers at the L.A. Coliseum. You might remember that game, as there were more than 100,000 fans in the stadium, which they had transformed from a football field into a makeshift baseball field. I had to stand in front of both teams' bullpens, which were set up next to each other, and talk into a camera halfway up the bleachers. Talk about nerve-wracking! There were also Hollywood celebrities standing nearby with field passes, since it was an exhibition game.

After I was hired at NESN, I would laugh with the producer and director about the circus atmosphere of my audition. But clearly I had passed the test, and after one more flight to Boston to meet with the network president and team owners, everyone signed off on hiring me. I moved 3,000 miles away from home, was greeted with a stack of books on the history of the Red Sox, and my "baseball TV" career was born.

"Undercover Operation in Vegas"

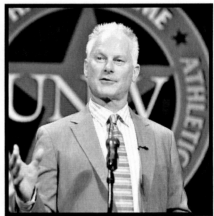

Photo Courtesy: UNLV Athletics

-From The Author:

Kenny Mayne is one-of-a-kind. This is not breaking news. But even after watching Kenny's work for all these years, first from across the country and then from across the building, I didn't realize just how original he really is. This chapter brought it all into focus. Hey, we are the sum of our experiences. And Kenny's are…well, distinctive. You need read only about five sentences to understand that his road to TV stardom was truly unlike any other.

Kenny Mayne

·KLVX, Las Vegas, NV   ·ESPN
·KSTW, Seattle, WA   ·NBC/Peacock

There I was with my 15-year-old vo-tech school photographer. The Las Vegas Strip. We were right outside the old Holiday Casino, across from Caesars Palace. I wore a wireless microphone. I thought I was Morley Safer. This was to be a big undercover investigation of prostitution in Las Vegas. I was doing journalism. Trouble is, we didn't hide the wireless mic very well. Allegedly, this young lady was a prostitute. I was just holding a conversation. She asked, "Do you want to party?"

Who knows what I said in response? Whatever it was didn't matter to her. She saw my mic and knew I was not Morley Safer. This wasn't *60 Minutes*. This was an inexperienced reporter in his final semester at UNLV, not exactly getting a ton of material for his investigative piece. She screamed, "What in the heck are you doing? You're wearing a microphone!"

It's all Lee Winston's fault.

He was the boss at KLVX, the local PBS affiliate. I was his paid intern. They'd sent a boy to do a man's job. And with the boy they sent another boy, my 15-year-old vo-tech photographer. Lee was the host of the station's community affairs program. That's the local PBS show that every market used to have. It would run on Sundays at like 3:00 p.m. The audience measurement was an asterisk.

My job, at $50 per story, was to put together a "set-up" story for Lee so he could then have a lengthier discussion with some expert about the topic. I did my own edits on those stories.

I was a horrible editor. Maybe even worse at editing than reporting. Sometimes I didn't make precise edits. Sometimes there were gaps in the edits resulting in a few frames of black on TV. The audio was worse. I didn't really know how to ride the levels. I think I checked out on that part of the instruction in Dr. Al Paderud's UNLV broadcasting classes. I knew I wanted to be the guy on camera, and not the guy who made the guy on camera look good. I should have paid attention.

The week in question was the week Lee was to delve into the world of prostitution in Las Vegas. And now I'm standing on the Vegas strip and an *alleged* prostitute is screaming at me because she spotted my wireless mic and caught on to my nervousness in my interaction with her. Even having spotted the mic she didn't seem to be worried. No, that was my photographer and me. In fact, we were so nervous, we just got the heck out of there. We hustled to our van, threw the equipment in the back, and drove off before an *alleged* pimp came for us. We hustled into the van so quickly, we left the tripod belonging to KLVX on the Las Vegas Strip. Presumably, the *alleged* prostitute was able to use that for a second career in photography. We had the task of explaining ourselves to the general manager at KLVX. But Lee stepped in and covered for us. I don't know what he said, but in the end we were treated like little kids who'd made a bad mistake. Both things were true.

A few days after we'd escaped with our lives (but without our tripod), I was approached by a new UNLV coach who'd come in with the new football staff after my senior season. He pulled me aside and tried to warn me about my "conduct." Turns out he held a part-time job at the casino we were standing near that night and had seen me with the *alleged* prostitute. He assumed I'd been trying to make a street transaction. I had to explain how I was doing journalism. I don't think he believed me.

I can't remember much about how that TV story turned out. I just know it was probably poorly told and poorly edited, but did include my getting screamed at outside the Holiday Casino. RIP Holiday Casino. And my substandard work for Lee Winston. As bad as I was at my job, Lee Winston always encouraged me. He told me to keep working at it. And I did.

I worked at it so much that I sort of worked my way out of another job I was holding at the same time. I was a horse race announcer for one of the two companies that piped in race calls to the sports books around Las Vegas. Back in those days, most of the tracks did not offer satellite feeds so the customers could watch an actual race. Instead, the race call companies hired people like me to recreate the calls for the customers who stood around in the race books and stared at a giant board with the names of the horses while listening to our calls. I wanted that job so badly.

For my first couple years at UNLV, I would go to the books to bet on horses with my running back friend, Ray Crouse. I was a backup QB and Ray was one of the main backs. We shared a love of football and horse racing. He grew up in the San Francisco Bay Area and used to go to Golden Gate Fields. I grew up near Seattle and went to Longacres. So before football meetings at 2:30 p.m., we'd drive up to one of the books and catch a couple of races. I listened to the announcers do their thing and knew I could do my version. I'd done it all my life—whether calling bike races, or while in the car with my parents (calling a mock race with other cars) or sometimes I'd make "race" calls using the names of girls in school. So I was prepared. The men in charge thought less of my ability when I approached them about a job opportunity. After some persistence, one of them let me come in for a tryout and I was hired on the spot. I was to be paid as much as $150 a week. I was rich. This worked out to about $1.51 an hour, but it was still $150. That was enough to keep my car on the road. It was a Fiat, which the mechanic told me stood for "fix it again Tony." He was right. My car was always in the shop for little things. A bigger thing was the radiator. It was going south. I didn't have enough money to replace it, so I just drove gas station to gas station when I went about town, filling it with water as needed.

So now I was a race caller and a television reporter. But those two would conflict and eventually the race call boss told me I couldn't keep making excuses for why I needed time off, or why I needed to come in a bit late or leave early for my TV job. He let me go, and I devoted that time to my horrible-looking TV stories for Lee Winston. Something else would then come up that had me walking away from the opportunity to make $50 per story for Lee's community affairs show.

The Seattle Seahawks wanted to know if my coach Tony Knap was lying to them.

Coach Knap had just retired at the end of my senior season in 1981. The kid who played ahead of me, Sam King, had led the nation in passing yards. He turned down a free-agent deal with the Seahawks, so Coach Knap told them that the guy behind Sam—me—wasn't all that far off from the guy they liked. So I headed up to Seattle for a tryout. Not in my Fiat. I can't even remember what I did with it. Did I sell it to a dealer? Abandon it on the side of the Strip? Give it to the *alleged* prostitute? Who knows? And who cares? I was going to throw for the Seattle Seahawks.

The day I arrived at their old HQ in Kirkland, Washington, to throw, one of the guys in the facility who was asked to come out and run routes for a tryout was this guy Steve Largent (Pro Football Hall of Famer). He caught everything and made me look OK. I signed on the spot. No bonus and something like $30,000 if I made the team. That was way more than $50 a story.

I worked out with some of the team at voluntary workouts before heading to camp in Cheney, WA. It was there, on the morning of the first workouts, that I was waived. They did some kind of strength test on me and it turned out my bad ankle (fractured/dislocated, 1980) was *very* bad. I failed the physical. An intern drove me to the airport and gave me an envelope. It was my airport meal money. Inside were a five-dollar bill, four ones, and four quarters. I made ten dollars in my NFL career.

I needed a job.

After about a week of what felt like the flu but was probably depression, I saw an ad in the newspaper. An independent TV station called KSTW was looking for college-educated broadcasting majors. This ad was talking to me. I called the news director, Jack Eddy, and he hired me over the phone.

I was going to make $6.55 an hour to work four hours a night, five nights a week. At the time, KSTW had a Monday-through-Friday news operation. The motto for the *Ten O'Clock News* was "an hour ahead of the rest." Another motto could have been, "If there's news on the weekends, it's news to us."

My job was to come in at 7:00 p.m., pull apart the five-way script copy, and get it distributed to the right people. The director used the green sheets, the producer the pink, etc.

That took about seven minutes. I'd then listen to the police and fire scanner and let the producer know if something big was going down. I answered phones. I sat around and did very little.

There were some who said if I intended to be on TV I should be applying in smaller markets. I *was* working for a small station, even though it was in the (top 15) Seattle-Tacoma market. But I was stubborn, and felt like my start should come right there. It took a while to convince others. Eventually, I moved up to writing for the anchors, and substituting as the *Ten O'Clock News* producer. They even let me go out and shadow the real reporters so I could see how it was done. I did some practice stories that didn't make air. A few years went by. It was looking grim. Maybe I should have started in Bend, Oregon, or somewhere like that after all.

But then Alice Blanchard quit.

She was a good reporter and always good to me with advice. By day, she was one of the news reporters, but at night she was going to law school. When she completed that, she gave notice at the station.

It was my good fortune that, at the time, the parent company of KSTW—Gaylord Broadcasting—had instituted a hiring freeze. Alice was leaving but they couldn't hire anyone. I was already hired. Jack Eddy called me in and told me I would make as much as $9.75 an hour. I was going to be a news reporter for KSTW. An hour ahead of the rest.

I think my first story was about a landfill that was leaking methane gas. What did they think landfills do?

But my second story I will never forget. I met STEVIE WONDER.

I talked the assignment editor into letting me drive up to Seattle for Stevie's sound check. He was kicking off his *In Square Circle* tour the next night. I viewed Stevie as both a genius and something of a prophet (I still do), and couldn't have been more excited to be in his presence. Excited and beyond nervous. We were allowed into the old Seattle Coliseum and were told we had 20 minutes to shoot video of his sound check, but Stevie would not be doing interviews. A more enterprising local reporter ignored the rules and walked up on stage during a break and started firing off questions. The rest of us hustled up to the stage and surrounded Stevie's electric piano and joined in. I was last in line and tried to reach my mic across his keys. My hand was shaking in the moment. I was just feet away from STEVIE WONDER. I laid my mic on his keys in the middle of an answer. His words were augmented by whatever notes I was playing. He didn't get mad. He didn't mention it. He turned the volume to zero. Years later I was able to tell him that "we collaborated that day."

Two days into my career as a TV reporter, I had (sort of) interviewed Stevie Wonder. I was making $9.75 an hour. Thank you, UNLV. Thank you, Al Paderud and Lee Winston.

I wanted to be in news or eventually documentaries. A show like PBS *Frontline* would have been my goal. But about a year later, KSTW decided to add weekend shows. Jack called me in and said, "You played football, you're doing sports." Against my will, I took the assignment. About two years later,

Joe Montana threw a TD to John Taylor and the 49ers beat the Bengals in the Super Bowl. I thought I had a pretty good show that night. I sent that tape to ESPN. A guy named Al Jaffe, then the talent recruiter, called me and said I should send another tape.

"We want to see if that one you sent was a fluke."

I sent another. And another. I got an interview but wasn't hired. For some reason I quit my KSTW job about six months later.

But I still pursued ESPN. That's a story for a different book.

"Yes, I *Did* Bleed for the Station"

-From The Author:

Steve Bunin is as good a writer as he is a softball player, and that's saying something. Like many of us, he navigated the traditional path from meager beginnings to the national TV spotlight. He then took a page out of my playbook, choosing to leave ESPN to help launch one of the Comcast SportsNet (now NBC Sports) regional networks (Houston). Steve also holds the rare distinction of once falling through his dining room floor, but that's another story entirely.

Steve Bunin

·WTVH, Syracuse, NY   ·ESPN
·WICZ, Binghamton, NY   ·Comcast SportsNet Houston
·KNAZ, Flagstaff, AZ   ·KFNC-FM, Houston, TX
·WLAJ, Lansing, MI   ·Yahoo Sports Radio
·WOTV, Battle Creek, MI   ·KING, Seattle, WA

"You never really bled for the station."

A good stock line if you're about to can somebody, except that "somebody" was me, and it overlooked the small detail that I had, *literally*, bled for the station. Oh, and that the guy doing the canning was the news anchor who threw to me for the sportscast that bloody night.

Looking back, I guess I should have been tipped off during my job interview a year prior that this wasn't the most professional outfit. It was the winter of 2000 at WLAJ-TV, the ABC affiliate and by far the least-watched station in Lansing, Michigan. That same news anchor (who doubled as the station's news director—in and of itself a warning sign that you're in Smallmarketsville) took me out to dinner. Having read my share of John Grisham novels, I was envisioning, if not a steak and lobster dinner, then at least a glass of red wine I'd fake like I knew how to smell properly.

Alas, this was no scene from an Italian restaurant...not even a checkerboard tablecloth pizzeria. No, the dinner portion of my job interview took place in a strip mall a few blocks away from the station at...wait for it...Blimpie, which has all the ambience its name suggests. It's a (small) step above Subway, if you have a proclivity for fluffier bread and larger cheese slices without all of the vegetable options. I think he did pick up the bill, though honestly I can't say for sure.

But who was I to complain? Heck, I was a 26-year-old sportscaster who'd been stuck in Flagstaff, Arizona, for two and a half years. Flagstaff is a beautiful city just an hour from the Grand Canyon, but with a population so small it doesn't even qualify as a TV market.

No, Blimpie in Lansing wasn't exactly the 5-star treatment. But I was desperate. I'd been stuck in northern Arizona for two and a half years. Don't get me wrong—I was grateful for that job when I got it, and looking back, it was a perfect place to learn and grow and improve, and it's a wonderful city that remains the favorite pre-ESPN stop of my career. But after your third year promoting the annual youth volleyball car wash fundraiser at the Fuddrucker's parking lot, ("*Parents—Sign up your kids on the way out of the Basha's grocery store! Jan, back to you for the weather!*"), you start to wonder whether your sportscasting dreams will ever come true...or if you'll even move up to a market as exciting as, say, Binghamton, New York.

Blimpie or not, I was pumped to be interviewing in Lansing. It was market #105! Making a 100-plus market jump was something I could hang my hat on. Moreover, the city actually played bigger than its market size, and not just because it's the capital of Michigan. For a sportscaster, what you're covering matters much more than the size of the city. In other words, even though Savannah, GA, ranks #89 and Gainesville, FL, ranks #156, it's better to cover the Florida Gators in the SEC than the (checks Wikipedia), Division Two Savannah State Tigers.

Lansing had lots of things Flagstaff didn't—a minor league baseball team (go Lugnuts!), for one. But mostly, it was Big Ten country, with an athletic program perhaps unrivaled in the country at the time. Michigan State's football, hockey, and men's basketball teams were all ranked in the top ten nationally, and Tom Izzo's "Flintstones" were a popular pick to buttress their 1999 Final Four appearance with a national title in 2000, Mateen Cleaves' senior season.

Blimpie? Big deal. I'd be vaulting from Little League to the Big Time. I'd eat a banana slug if it got me the job. And I did (get the job, not eat a banana slug).

Right off the bat, it was a dream come true. On April 3, 2000, about a month after I arrived in town, Michigan State beat Florida to win the men's basketball national championship. As working press, I literally had a front-row seat to all the action. When Mateen Cleaves cut down the net, I was near the ladder. As "One Shining Moment" played on the big board, I was standing on the court next to Magic Johnson. In the postgame scrum in the bowels of the RCA Dome, I asked the first question to Tom Izzo. This was a million miles from Flagstaff. Life. Was. Good.

But about a week later, life wasn't so good. I broke my nose badly in a pickup basketball game, going up for a rebound and smashing into a high-flying opponent's knee (turns out, kneecaps are stronger than nasal bones). I crumpled to the ground, and when I opened my eyes, I had the odd experience of feeling blood gushing down my nose, but seeing a small puddle of red about a foot in front of me. You see, his knee had also opened up a gash between my eyes, which was squirting blood outward like a mini-hose. Good times. An hour or so later, a plastic surgeon snapped my nose mostly back into place, using the age-old, "I'll do it on three" trick, where they actually do it on two.

A rhinoplasty the next day left me looking as good as new, other than two massive black eyes. Makeup couldn't cover them up sufficiently, but I could type and edit video, so I didn't take any time off. I suggested doing a week of "video sports"—voicing the sportscast live without actually appearing on the air. It wasn't ideal, but I was trying to prove myself. I'd only been on the job about six weeks, and for three of them, I'd spent considerable time on the road covering MSU's tournament run. So I felt a lot of pressure to physically be at the station. One reason: there was nobody else in the WLAJ sports department, so if *I* wasn't on-air, nobody was.

But even the bloody nose that left me feeling like an extra in the movie *Braveheart* isn't what I meant when I said I bled for the station. No, that came a few weeks later, on Wednesday, May 10, 2000.

That evening, before our 6:00 p.m. newscast, I noticed my right quadriceps seemed swollen and abnormally stiff to the touch...like trying to press on a table, I remember thinking. I wasn't too worried—until I went to the bathroom to check it out. It was red. Dark red. And hot to the touch. Not warm—hot. That seemed...alarm-worthy. So I limped to the studio, did the 6:00 p.m. sportscast, and drove off to Ingham Medical Center.

Long story short, I was diagnosed with cellulitis—not to be confused with extra padding in your midsection, thank you very much. That's cellulite. Turns out cellulitis it is a serious bacterial infection that, if left untreated, can lead to amputation or death. It's usually the result of a blunt injury or bug bite (though I had no evidence of either).

They immediately stuck an IV needle in my arm, got me on the proper medication, and said they had to give me another round in eight hours, but no sooner. Other than the leg, though, I felt fine, so I asked, can I leave the hospital and come back at 3:00 a.m.? First of all, there were no cellphones then, so what was I gonna do, stare at the ceiling for eight hours? But more importantly, there was nobody else in the sports department at WLAJ, so who else was going to anchor the 11:00 p.m. sportscast? Keep in mind—I'd just done the whole "video-sports" routine, which is not actually a thing in our industry. The last thing I wanted was any MORE reason for my new colleagues to question my commitment.

"Sure," they said at the hospital. "You can leave the premises, but we're not poking you again. The IV needle stays in."

"Fine by me," I said.

They capped off the needle, and I drove back to the TV station. Here's the thing—nobody lying in bed at 11:23 p.m. wants to see an IV needle dangling out of a sportscaster's arm when he's doing Lansing Lugnut highlights, and I didn't want to bring back "video sports." So I proposed a different workaround, which will sound simple enough now, but at the time was pretty revolutionary for market #105. I'd anchor the sportscast from inside the newsroom (as a live reporter might do, to front their story), and they'd simply zoom in so the viewer could only see my head, neck and shoulders. It wasn't the same as being on the anchor desk in studio, but it meant I didn't have to try to slip my arm/needle through the sleeve of a suit.

It went fine on the air.

At midnight, I drove back to the hospital, got my next round of intravenous fluids, and went home with a boatload of pain meds (epilogue: the pain meds started tearing away at the lining of my stomach, and a few days later, I was in excruciating stomach pain and bleeding profusely from an area you can guess but I don't want to say, so I drove back to the hospital, where I stayed for eight days, having contracted C.difficile, a colitis that, had it not been treated properly, could have killed me).

But I was lucky. I had health insurance, I had good doctors, I was 26 and otherwise healthy (I mean, besides the weird leg thing and the broken nose). I recovered, and as spring turned to summer and then fall, I was hitting my stride at WLAJ. I worked six-day weeks almost the entire year, even though we had no weekend newscasts (tip for bosses at TV stations that don't cover news on two of the seven days in the week: don't hold it against your employees when you are consistently last in the ratings). But weekend newscasts or not, sports— especially big-time NCAA football and basketball games, but also plenty of high school events—happen on Saturdays.

I worked Saturdays all that autumn and winter as the calendar turned to 2001. As the one person in a one-person department, I shot many of those prep and college games, then spent countless lonely hours meticulously logging the video, so I could later find that important yet elusive Plaxico Burress catch or Charlie Bell assist for the rest of my career in Lansing.

Turns out, it wouldn't be long. That winter, to combat our bad ratings, management decided to do "Turbo News," where we'd jam all the news, weather and sports into the "A-block" (the first 10-minute segment of the newscast), allowing the final 20 minutes to delve into a single topic, *Nightline* style. Kudos for trying something different than the competitors, but we had neither *Nightline's* resources behind the camera, nor the talented news anchor on-camera, to pull it off. It didn't last long.

It also meant, instead of the usual three minutes for a sportscast (already a short sliver of time), I only had 60 seconds to cram all of my content on the air. In a sports-loving city like Lansing, you just can't do it. It takes at least 15 seconds to give even a cursory amount of information on a single topic, and the average sound bite is about 15 seconds, so you tell me how to fit stories about Michigan State football and basketball, high school sports, minor league baseball, University of Michigan athletics, and the Detroit pro sports scene (let alone a big national story) into 60 seconds. It simply cannot be done. Viewers will be shortchanged and tune to somebody else.

Then, that February, I got a parking ticket in a news vehicle while covering a high school basketball game, which wasn't something I'd put on my resume, but seemed innocuous enough. I would have forgotten it, but for what happened the next month.

From March 15-18, 2001, I was in Memphis, covering the first two rounds of the Spartan basketball team's title defense. By the ensuing Monday, I was planning the itinerary for the Sweet 16 and Elite 8 in Atlanta. I came into work and thought nothing of it when I was told to go to the boss's office. I figured he'd ask me to finalize the details of the trip, and maybe make preliminary plans for covering the Final Four in Minneapolis.

Here's a tip for you young people out there in any industry: If you ever walk into the boss's office and nothing is on their desk except for a single envelope? You're about to get fired.

I don't remember the entire conversation word-for-word, but I remember that he brought up the parking ticket (as if that was a fireable offense), and I *vividly* remember him defending his decision, saying, "You never really bled for the station." What. In. The. Actual.

Remember, this news director was also our news anchor, so he was the one who had exchanged witty banter with me on-air the night I did the 11:00 p.m. sportscast WITH AN I.V. NEEDLE LITERALLY POKING OUT OF MY ARM!!! I had LITERALLY bled for the station!

Of course, I knew then and know now that he meant it as in, I never gave 100%. But that was equally inaccurate and even more hurtful. I was the only station employee who'd toiled away all those Saturdays despite not having a weekend newscast, not to mention how hard I had worked on weekdays as the only person in the sports department. Producing, writing, and anchoring every sportscast our station did, and shooting events five to six days a week. Didn't bleed for the station? That one cut like a knife, and not in a Bryan Adams sort of way.

I subsequently went a year and a half without landing another TV gig, moving back home with Mom and Dad and being rejected from such sports meccas as Zanesville, Ohio and many, many, many more. I honestly thought my career might be over, until I was finally rescued by a TV station that was run out of a former military barracks in Battle Creek, Michigan. So you'd better believe, a year after that, when I got the call from ESPN, I shed a lot of tears. That day and many since, I've thought of the man who said I never bled for the job, and wondered if he even remembers. If he does, I hope he feels as remorseful and ridiculous in retrospect as I feel proud.

"There's an Opening in Visalia"

-From The Author:

Dave Flemming tells stories of small-market lunacy, but from a different perspective: that of a play-by-play announcer rather than a sports anchor. His journey illustrates the parallels between the two tracks, but also details experiences that are very much indigenous to that particular world, centered around the ballpark instead of the studio. Dave is a fellow Stanford alum (shout out to KZSU!) and has three more World Series rings than the rest of us combined.

Dave Flemming

·**Bakersfield Blaze**   ·**Stanford Football/Basketball**
·**Visalia Oaks**   ·**San Francisco Giants**
·**Pawtucket Red Sox**   ·**ESPN**

My first job in baseball was in Visalia, California. Actually, that's not true. My first job was in Bakersfield, a hot and dusty hour south of Visalia on Highway 99. I signed up to spend the 2000 minor league baseball season as the unpaid broadcast intern for the Bakersfield Blaze, a job I chose over a paid offer from the Idaho Falls Padres. Those Padres only played 70 games in a season, whereas the Blaze had a full schedule of 140 games. I needed the experience, so I headed to the Central Valley. Bakersfield promised me meal money and a place to stay, and I figured I could make that work.

The Blaze had been around a long time, since 1941. The team actually had some amazing history—the Dodgers fielded a team in Bakersfield for many years, and players like Ron Cey, Steve Garvey, Mike Piazza, and Pedro Martinez all came through on their way to big league stardom. They played their games at Sam Lynn Ballpark, the oldest park for pro baseball in California. Whoever Sam Lynn was might have been a good guy, but the ballpark that carried his name was a dump.

The biggest issue was not the dilapidated locker rooms, the moldy showers, or the dugouts with rotted wooden steps. Those were inconveniences. The biggest problem was that Sam Lynn built his ballpark with home plate facing due west. Every night, the sun would set directly in the eyes of the hitters. Directly. Because it was deemed impossible to lift the entire

57

ballpark and rotate it 90 degrees clockwise, the ball club started games at 7:00 p.m., and then some time in the first inning or two, stopped the games and waited for the sun to go down. After a 20-minute delay every night, play resumed. It didn't make for a good player or fan experience. By the 2000 season, the Blaze eliminated the delay and just resigned to starting games at 8:00 p.m.

But I never had to deal with those late-night games. I lasted in Bakersfield for a month, just long enough to survive a massive ant infestation in the Parkway Inn room where the team had stashed me. Nine days before the season began, a group of investors bought the Visalia Oaks, another California League club, and asked me to broadcast their games. They offered me a salary, and the title of broadcaster/assistant general manager. How could I turn that down? So I packed my stuff and headed north to Visalia.

If Bakersfield had been considered perhaps the worst franchise in minor league baseball, the Oaks were in the running for second place. Visalia's home was Recreation Park, a 1946 ballpark with the smallest seating capacity in the minor leagues, and even less charm. Rec Park featured the absolute bare minimum required to host a professional team. There were two spartan locker rooms with old metal lockers. There were some bleachers and a chain link backstop. And that was it. The Oaks didn't even own a tarp. That spring, we had a rare April rainstorm. The entire weekend of games was washed out—no tarp meant the infield turned into a quagmire that took days to dry out.

Part of the nuance of my distinguished title of "assistant general manager" was that the broadcasts were just a small slice of my duties. I painted walls and paid bills. After each home game, when the broadcast ended and the players and coaches cleared out, I would vacuum each clubhouse carpet and take out the trash. On the rare nights that we had a crowd bigger than a couple hundred, I'd step out of the booth for a half-inning and help change a keg in the concession stand behind home plate. There were only three of us working for the team; I had to do my part, and then some.

I probably shouldn't use the term booth—we didn't have a broadcast booth per se. There was a concrete bunker at the top of the stands that housed the PA microphone and music system. Prior to my season in Visalia, the broadcast originated from a folding table in the back row with no cover up above. I did use my assistant GM powers and confiscated some of the public address announcer's space in the bunker for our broadcast position. Unfortunately, the road announcers still had to work from the card table. That was the best we could do. It's so hot in central California in the summer that we almost never played day games, so at least the visiting guys avoided sitting out in the sun.

Our players were generally a decent group. That season Visalia was an Oakland A's affiliate. Ultimately seven of our players made it to the big leagues—that's a big number for an A-ball team. Our shortstop, Angel Berroa, was the American League rookie of the year in 2003. He made about 40 errors in 2000 for the Oaks, which gives you an idea of how even the most talented players have a lot of work to do when they are in the California League.

I got a pretty immediate clue that baseball in the minor leagues was not quite like the Orioles games I had grown up watching with my dad and my brother. Opening night for the Oaks was April 6, 2000, in Adelanto, CA. The Oaks against the High Desert Mavericks. Visalia trailed the game 9-2 in the ninth inning. Two out, no one on base. Ten batters later we led 10-9! Two hits, six walks, a hit batter, and eight runs. At one point during the rally, High Desert pitchers threw 23 of 26 pitches for balls. It was the craziest inning I had ever seen in my life. And then we coughed up two runs in the bottom of the ninth and lost anyway, 11-10. Minor league baseball!

One of the Oaks who eventually made it to the big leagues was a pitcher named Eric DuBose. He was a very funny and charismatic guy. When he first joined the team and met me, I was wearing a Stanford baseball T-shirt. He looked at the shirt and asked, "Are you a Stanford fan?"

"Yes," I said.

"You go there?" he asked.

"Yep." Eric burst into real laughter. He was howling. I asked him what was so funny.

He looked me dead in the eye and said, "You didn't need to go to Stanford! Heck, you didn't need to go to college! You're the darn radio guy!"

"Radio guy" is the universal term for a broadcaster in the minor leagues. In the last decade, there have thankfully been more young women who broadcast baseball in the minors. I imagine even most of them are called "radio guy." That's the term. It's not usually uttered with a huge serving of respect or admiration.

In Visalia, we would typically have a lug nut bet on bus rides. Each of us would pick numbers, and when the bus stopped, whichever lug nut on the front wheel of the bus ended up closest to 12 o'clock on the wheel was the winner of the pot. I think my number came up on the second trip of the year. I was pumped—that was $50! Wayne Nix, a starting pitcher on the team, barked as we got off the bus, "We gotta change the rules; the frickin' radio guy can't win."

I did think of Eric's declaration of my over-education often that season. My Stanford friends were off making six-figure salaries for consulting firms, or riding the wave of the first dot-com boom, or laughing through beer and softball nights at law school. I felt like I was a long, long way from anything like that. Our clubbie—the guy who washed the uniforms and prepared the meager clubhouse food spread—quit in the middle of a late May road trip. Just walked out. We needed to find a new clubbie, but in the meantime, I was on the road trip and I'd step in and do the job until the team made it back to Visalia. So I spent a week going to Albertson's in the afternoon as opposed to preparing for a broadcast. I'd buy a watermelon and a cantaloupe and some bread and peanut butter, and when I got to the ballpark, I'd slice the melons and slap together PB&J sandwiches. It was the best I could do.

That part of being a clubbie I didn't mind. The uniform washing was a different matter. We happened to be in Lake Elsinore, a desert town north of Temecula. Minor league teams often make an arrangement with the hotel where they stay that allows the team to use the hotel washers and dryers. They are industrial size and can handle the job. But these hotels only allow the machines to be used in the overnight hours when the housekeeping staff is gone. So after the game, I'd trudge back to the Lake Elsinore Hotel and Casino, go to the bar in the casino and order a cup of coffee. At about 2:00 a.m. I was allowed to haul the bags of laundry into the back room behind the front desk and start washing. One of those nights, May 30 turned into May 31. I was so bleary-eyed I hardly noticed. But I spent the first hours of my 24th birthday washing jockstraps and socks in the utility room of a two-bit casino.

That's the night I remember most vividly when I think to myself that I have things pretty licked as a big league broadcaster. Partly I remind myself that it doesn't always have to be this good. And partly I remind myself that I did sacrifice, work hard, and climb my way up the ladder to get a much more glamorous job. It wasn't handed to me.

That season flew by. The Oaks made the California League playoffs with a 78-62 record. We vanquished my "first" team, Bakersfield, in the opening round. Then we beat another A's affiliate, Modesto, in a winner-take-all game five by throwing a combined no-hitter! In true minor league fashion, the Oaks booted a couple balls, walked half a dozen, and gave up a run, but didn't allow a single hit! My first year in baseball came to an inglorious end when the San Bernardino Stampede swept us in the championship series.

That winter, the Pawtucket Red Sox hired me, so I moved to Rhode Island and up to Triple-A. Two years later, the San Francisco Giants asked me to do a handful of games, and by 2004 I was a big leaguer for good. This past season was my 19th as a major league broadcaster.

One of the minority owners of the Visalia Oaks was a gentleman named Pat Gallagher. He was a longtime and beloved front office member of the Giants. When the Giants needed that young announcer in 2003, Pat remembered listening to Oaks games on a crackly AM radio station on his drives into town, and told the Giants to make sure they gave this "Flemming kid" a listen.

At the end of the great baseball movie *Bull Durham*, Crash Davis was staring at the end of his playing career, and his own skipper thought he'd make a good manager himself. He said to Davis, "There might be an opening in Visalia next year." I'd like to think that Crash Davis took him up on that offer, and maybe that little town of Visalia did for him what it did for me.

"Sweating on New Year's Eve"

Photo Courtesy: WAVY

-From The Author:

Stan Verrett and I share a pretty significant anniversary: September 4, 2000. Both our first days at ESPN. I lasted eight years, while Stan is still going strong. He has been one of the faces of SportsCenter Los Angeles since its inception in 2009, and his golf game has improved exponentially since the big move to a California climate. A New Orleans native, it remains unclear whether Stan now considers himself more of a "Southerner" or a "Southern Californian."

Stan Verrett

·Magic 101.7 FM, Charleston, SC   ·WVEC, Norfolk, VA

·Z93 FM, Charleston, SC   ·WDSU, New Orleans

·WAVY, Norfolk, VA   ·ESPN

Before I got into television, I had a totally separate career in radio. Not sports radio, music radio. It actually goes back to my college days at Howard. I worked at a radio station during that time, and a consultant, who also consulted for a station in Charleston, South Carolina, told me he had a full-time job open there and, "If you want it, you got it."

So I packed up everything I had in my Volkswagen Jetta and drove down to Charleston, where I had never spent a day in my life. I started out DJ-ing evenings from 6:00-10:00 p.m. on Magic 101.7. Shortly thereafter, I transitioned to the morning show with a woman named Carolyn Murray, who is now a TV anchor in Charleston.

We were both young and energetic, and had a pretty good show. Apparently, it was good enough that the owner of one of the competitors in the market—Z93—started to get concerned about us. So he decided to poach me away from 101.7 with a better offer.

I took the job at Z93, which was about a $7,000 pay increase. That was big money, considering my initial salary was $17,000. To go from 17K to 24K, I felt like I had really made it.

I started doing "afternoon drive" there...did that for a while, and then moved back to mornings. Things were going well.

Z93 was #1 in the market despite having a very weak broadcast signal, not ideal for FM radio. That left us vulnerable to competition, and it just so happened there were three local stations that were in the process of switching their format to urban (hip hop and R&B) to challenge Z93. Within just a few months, Charleston had *four* urban radio stations, in a market of only a half-million people. And those three converted stations were broadcasting a signal between 25,000 and 50,000 watts. Z-93 broadcast at 6,000 watts. It wasn't even close.

So we had to be so good that basically everybody who *could* hear us would listen to us instead of the other stations. We survived on superior programming and better talent. We were just a better run station.

Then the owner of Z93 put in an application with the Federal Communications Commission (FCC) to increase his wattage to 50,000, to be on par with the competition. All the while, he was paying his employees more than market value, because he knew the station had to perform at a high level to compete. Well, he got the FCC approval to move up to 50,000 watts, then he fired the entire staff and hired a bunch of people who were cheaper.

I remember getting a call from the owner on a Sunday— which was really weird—telling me to come into the station. I walked in and all I remember is the woman who did the news on our morning show, Stephanie Gaines, yelling, "We've all been fired!" with tears streaming down her face.

I was like, "OK, I guess this explains the Sunday meeting."

Here's the thing. It was the only time I'd ever been fired. People tell you it's going to happen to you if you get into this business. They say you've got to learn from it, grow from it, and keep moving.

But it really, really rocked me. I felt like I was doing everything possible to keep the station operating at a high level. I was 25 years old when I became the operations director, the #2 in command, at a station involved in a ratings battle, and I led the station through that ratings battle. I felt like it was unfair that I got fired, but I swore I was going to make it work for me. I was going to plant the seeds to make sure this never happened again.

I'd always felt like I could work harder, do more, and make myself more valuable. A lot of that goes back to when I was in college. I was a "B" student with "A" ability. My mom would remind me of this all the time. So I promised myself that going forward in my career I would never settle for B's. I would make sure I had "A" ability by developing the skills, and once I had "A" ability I would never half-ass it. I was always going to do my best.

I was out of work for five months. I spent that time sending out resume tapes for radio jobs, spending time with friends, and reading motivational books. I put a ton of thought into how I wanted my career to play out. I felt like radio was a young man's business, and once I got to 30 or so I wouldn't want to do it anymore. And that was entrenched in the back of my mind, even as I took another radio job as morning DJ on 103 Jams in Norfolk, VA.

After that move, I sat down with a piece of paper and asked myself, "OK, what are my options?" There was radio, and I put that in one column, with pros and cons. I could go back to graduate school and get my MBA or law degree, so that was in another column. Or, I could get into television.

The first thing to do was create the option to actually pursue any of those things. That meant taking the LSAT and the GMAT, the entrance exams for law school and business school. Once I got settled in Norfolk, I decided to just do it.

I took an LSAT prep course and a GMAT prep course, then took both exams. I scored in the 89th percentile on the LSAT and the 90th percentile on the GMAT. I could have gone anywhere for law school or business school. But once I did another "pros and cons" assessment, I decided that TV was what I really wanted to do.

As luck would have it, that's when I met Barbara Sierra.

Barbara was the main news anchor at the local CBS affiliate. I was at a party one night at her house, and she asked me whether I had ever considered getting into TV. "Yeah, I have," I told her. "I've been having so much fun doing radio that I figured I'd just roll with that for a while. But now I think I am ready to make the transition to television."

"OK," she said, "I have a friend who can help you with that. He's going to give you a call."

I expected the friend to be someone from the CBS affiliate, but it turned out to be Bruce Radar, the sports director at the NBC affiliate. Bruce called me a couple of days later.

"Listen, Barbara tells me you're interested in getting into TV. I know you do the radio show," he said. "I don't have a position right now. Might have one in the future. But you can come by, we can talk and figure out how we can do something."

They didn't have a job for me, per se. I wasn't in college, so there was no way to do an internship, but I said I basically wanted to do an internship anyway. I just wanted to come by the station, hang around, learn how to be a sportscaster, and get the process started so that if there were a position in the future, I'd be ready.

Bruce allowed me to do just that, and I decided I was going to treat this as a full-time job, to really apply myself and make the break from radio into TV. Radio was fun while it lasted as a "young guy," but as I got older, I wanted something different. Deep down, television had always been my ultimate goal—once I got done with my young, rowdy years, that is. It was time.

I went to the station every day. I would do my radio show in the morning from 6:00 a.m. until 10:00 a.m., go home and take a nap, then go into the TV station at 3:00 p.m. and stay until the late news was finished at 11:30. I simply soaked up everything that was happening and talked as much as I could to different reporters and anchors. Meanwhile, all the people who knew me from radio would see me out and ask, "Hey man, when are they gonna put you on TV?"

"As soon as I get some skills," I would tell them. "But I don't have them right now."

This went on for several months. I learned how to edit and learned how to use the computer system. And in November, Bruce Radar told me to start making "practice tapes."

"Every Saturday, after the six p.m. news goes off the air, your show starts at six thirty-five," he told me. "Your sports show is five minutes long. You have to write and edit your own show and be ready to go at six thirty-five. The show director normally goes on his dinner break at six thirty-five, but he's agreed to do this as a favor to me by staying the extra ten minutes. Now, at six-thirty, if you're not ready to go, the camera is going to black, we're gonna see color bars and hear tone, because that's what would happen If you were really on the air. You need to treat this as if you're actually doing the sportscast on the six o'clock news."

So, every Saturday I would go into the studio at 6:35 p.m. and do my sportscast. I treated it like it was *SportsCenter*. Bruce would look at my tape on Monday and tell me what I needed to work on. I would process that during the week, watch how other anchors went about their business, and then come Saturday I'd repeat the drill.

In December, 1994, the "number three" sports guy at the station got a job in Washington, D.C. Which meant a job was opening up and I needed to work on those tapes with a little more urgency. The holiday season in TV news means lots of "fill-in" opportunities, and come Christmas Eve, I could be on the air.

The week before Christmas, I did what I hoped would be my final "practice" run. The news director looked at it and said bluntly, "No, you're not ready." I gave Bruce the bad news, but Bruce wasn't having it.

"Look," said Bruce, "the weekend guy is on vacation next week, and I'm not coming in on Christmas Eve. Let me go talk to him." He came back to me later that day and said, "OK, you're gonna be on Friday, be ready to go!"

All of a sudden, it was GO time.

Christmas Eve, 1994, on WAVY-TV in Norfolk, Virginia, I made my big debut. And everything went great. People called me at the station, telling me I was a natural, I was so good at this. And honestly for a first show, it *was* really good.

The thing was, on that day there was only an 11:00 p.m. newscast, so I had all day to get ready for just one show. Christmas night, same thing. I had only one show, lots of football on, it was relatively easy.

The next weekend, I was on again. But this time it was New Year's Eve, and we had the more customary two newscasts—6:00 p.m. and 11:00 p.m. I got through the 6:00 okay, but it was December 31 and there were a whole bunch of bowl games later in the day. At this point in my young career, I could edit and could produce a show, but not under fire. And with all those games I had to get into the show, I was very much under fire. So I decided to edit 30 seconds of highlights from each game and then go back later and put in the information I would need to read the highlights. Well, I got the tapes edited, but I never got around to getting the information for my scripts before we went on the air. So I had no choice but to "ad-lib" the highlights. In no way was I equipped to do that.

I remind you, this was my third time ever on television. I did not have those skills.

My sportscast was five minutes long. The first three minutes were NFL highlights and post-game reaction I had already done at 6:00 p.m., so that would all be fine. I then had two minutes remaining for four 30-second bowl game highlights, with absolutely no information in my script.

As I'm making my way through the NFL highlights, I begin sweating profusely, because I know I have absolutely no idea what I'm going to do when I get to those college games. We get there, and I pop on camera for a quick "lead-in" to the Bowl games. And I am drenched in sweat. They roll the first highlight tape, and I can't even make out which teams are playing. Like, "It's Syracuse against Georgia Tech—no wait, this is Illinois and Georgia." It's a total disaster.

As I continue to ramble and sweat, the director figures out that I have no idea what's going on. He gets in my ear and actually asks, "Do you know what's happening here?" I shake my head "no." He says, "OK, we are gonna bail out of this."

So he brings me back on camera, and I say simply, "That's a look at sports."

I am drenched. The news anchor looks at me and says, "Thanks, Stan. We'll be right back." We go to commercial break and I feel like the worst human being in the world. I've failed, my career is over, nobody is ever going to put me back on TV after this.

To make matters worse, since I didn't get through the final 90 seconds of highlights, there was a big "hole" at the end of the newscast. So the producer in the control room calls the news reporter—who had been live from downtown earlier in the show—and tells her, "We need you to come back on after the commercial for another report to help us eat up some time, because sports went light."

A reminder, this was New Year's Eve. The reporter and her photographer had already wrapped for the night (so they thought), lowered the mast from the live truck (which is a process), and were hoping to make it to a party by midnight to ring in the new year. Now, they had to go back to work because of my screwup. So they're not happy with me because I've made it virtually impossible for them to get to their party on time. I feel like I pretty much let the whole team down.

Fortunately, if this had to happen, it happened on the perfect night. I mean, who is watching the news at 11:00 p.m.

on New Year's Eve? Almost nobody. People are out; and if they *are* home watching TV, they're watching *New Year's Rockin' Eve* or something like that. It was a safe bet that hardly anybody actually witnessed my horror.

But that didn't stop me from going to a party later that night and asking everybody I saw, "You didn't happen to watch *Channel 10 News at 11:00*, did you?". As it turned out, the only person I could find who actually watched was the girlfriend of one of my buddies.

"Yeah," she said. "It didn't really look like you had your stuff together." I said, "OK. Don't tell anybody!"

That was my second weekend on the air.

Looking back, I know I wasn't prepared. It wasn't out of neglect or laziness. It was because I didn't have the skills to do everything I needed to do as a one-man sports department in the time I was allotted to do it. But I decided that night, I was going to use this as a "scared straight" moment. *This is what happens when you go on the air unprepared*, and I don't ever want to feel like that again. I felt like a total failure, like I had blown it—like if there had been a large audience for that show, if it had been any night besides New Year's Eve, that could have been really destructive. It could have really killed my confidence if people had come up to me saying, "Hey I saw that show, you were awful!"

So my confidence wasn't killed, but it was crippled. For about the next six months, I was literally terrified of going on TV. I would get almost physically ill as the show got closer.

But ultimately it became a seminal experience. It motivated me to become a stickler for preparation, and it still serves me to this day. I make sure I am always prepared. I will over-prepare sometimes, but I am never going to allow myself to be in a situation where I'm on the air, that red light comes on, and I am not 100% ready.

Looking back, that was a rough period. I mean, it was really, really tough. But I'm glad it happened, because the lesson it taught me is one that really stuck, and has guided me throughout my career.

"The Hawaiian Van Halen Fanboy"

Photo Courtesy: KGMB

-From The Author:

    Neil Everett is Stan's partner in Los Angeles, essentially because ESPN has yet to commission a studio in Hawaii. Neil is unabashedly unique, a quality which I hold in the highest regard when it comes to sports anchors. There are just so many of us out there, all telling the same stories and reading the same highlights. It's really hard to be unique. Neil is also as authentic as they come—the guy you see on TV is exactly the guy you meet in person—and I am confident the pages ahead will entertain, but not surprise, his faithful viewers.

Neil Everett

·**KCST-FM, Florence, OR** ·**KGMB, Honolulu, HI**
·**Hawaii Pacific University** ·**KHNL, Honolulu, HI**
·**KITV, Honolulu, HI** ·**ESPN**

I shouldn't be here...at least not the way I got here. My first job in television was not in sports, and being a sportscaster wasn't something I ever dreamed about. Living in Hawaii in the mid-1980s, I needed to make some extra money. I was a full-time sports information director at Hawaii Pacific University. But that paycheck wasn't cutting it with Hawaii's high cost of living. So I started reaching out to the three local television stations on Oahu. I knew I could write, and again, I knew I needed the money. The three news directors kept giving me the lukewarm shoulder but I kept on 'em. Wore 'em down. Eventually, a fella named Paul Udell, the news director at KITV (the ABC affiliate), relented. "C'mon down, we will find something for you."

That "something" was writing copy for the 10:00 p.m. newscast...news copy. The lead anchor loved how I livened up her scripts with sports phrases or action verbs. I just loved having a job—two jobs, mind you. I would work at the college from the morning into the late afternoon, then go to KITV to do my thing. When HPU had a night game, I was unavailable at the TV station, but for the most part, it was a 60-plus-hour work week. Not complaining, because I loved the juice in a newsroom: Deadlines...writing...live television.

Then one week Mr. Udell had himself a problem. One of his sportscasters was out sick and the other was on vacation. He had no one to do the sports on that weekend's newscast.

"Hey Neil," he says, "Don't you do something with sports in your other job?"

I'm like, "Yeah, I'm a sports information director."

"Good enough for me," he says. "You're doing the sports this weekend."

I'd never been on the air. I still have the VHS tape of that first night. Paula Akana was the news anchor's name...shared the same May 18th birthday with me...she was so kind. I was bedecked in leis—that's how it's done in the Aloha State. Big smile on my face like I'd won something big. I was more pumped than nervous...pulled it off...did the weekend shows, and then went back to my regular writing gig.

Eventually I was shifted from associate producer to weekend assignment editor. It's kind of a thankless job, telling reporters and camera folks what to cover. Sure, some of 'em had regular "beats," but I remember one time I had to decide which photographer was going to cover Van Halen's rehearsal. This was the first time VH had been to Hawaii...it was a big deal. I, of course, assigned myself to do the reporting...the desk would be fine without me for a while!

I chose a dude named Eric Nolder to be the cameraman, and that did not go over that well with Fred Asmus, another cameraman. Fred and I are dear friends to this day. I didn't know him as well back then or I would have picked him. Nolder was tall and I thought I might need tall...don't know why. So we go to the Blaisdell (event complex in Honolulu) where VH is doing its sound check. I'm interviewing Alex Van Halen (drummer) and Michael Anthony (bassist). All of a sudden I notice Fred is there, too! He's filming me being filmed by Eric, which was good for two reasons. First, we were the only station there, because I

was the only one hip enough to want VH in the show...secondly, it ended up being a two-camera shoot which looked big-time! I still have the story on a 3/4 inch tape...need to figure out how to put that on DVD so I can see what a fanboy I was!

Later in my Hawaii life, I found myself at KGMB (CBS affiliate), where I actually switched places with the late Robert Kekaula, who went to KITV. At KGMB, I was named the sports director, but was told I'd be doing the weekend shows. Basically, they liked my leadership in the "sports cave," but preferred that another guy represent on the set during the week. It was their station, so I had to swallow my pride a bit.

The story I remember is Robert calling me and asking me to join him at the "new" station. KHNL is now the NBC affiliate, but was an independent back then. I loved the idea of working with Robert. He was large and in-charge, local, garnered a lot of respect in the "808"...I knew I could roll with him...and have some fun. We did. I still remember a mini-golf segment we did...another one of those gems I have on VHS somewhere in my garage. Robert passed away in July of 2021. I'm kicking myself that I didn't stay in better touch.

Anyway, Robert and I were the sports team at KHNL...I was still working my Hawaii Pacific job, but only part-time...television was my thing.

My old boss at HPU asks me if I can do play-by-play on TV for the basketball team. The station carrying it was waaaaaaaaaaaaay off the dial...I think it was a religious station the school bought time on. I loved doing play-by-play, so I was all in. The local newspaper runs a story on it...then I get called into the principal's office at KHNL. They tell me I've violated my contract by agreeing to do the play-by-play for another station, saying it's a direct competitor. I told 'em they needed to raise their standards and adjust their self-esteem if they thought that station was a competitor. They fired me. I hadn't been there six months.

What I think happened was, they brought in a consultant (failed television fella) who did not dig my look and/or style. Granted, I did have an awful mustache back then, so the story in the paper was their way of dumping me so they could hire a kid who looked way better than I did. I sued 'em for firing me. I came out on the right side of that judgment, but it took over a year and I almost left Hawaii because I could not get another gig on the tube. Heck, I applied to be the spokesperson for the wastewater treatment plant...and didn't get the job. I struck out to be the sh*t spokesman...that was a low blow.

I had to make something happen, so I flew to Portland for an informal job search at Nike, thanks to my sister, who was a Nike big shot. Then I'm on Hawaiian Air heading home to Oahu, bemoaning that I gotta move back to the Mainland…and they play a video of Henry Kapono singing, "Home in the Islands." At that moment I tell myself, you gotta find a job to stay in Hawaii!

Just so happens, that week I get two calls: one from KGMB, my old homies, and the other from the folks at KHON (NBC) who want me to be a news producer-type and work with the legendary Joe Moore. Dude might still be there and this was 25-30 years ago. KGMB wanted me to come back and just be a "rover" do-it-all type in the newsroom, and that's the job I took. Don Rockwell was the news director's name. He tells me, "Just find a story and go do it...or when we need you on a story, we'll send you." So I was back in the game!

Mr. Rockwell must have moved on, because it was a different dude in charge when I got my biggest break, thanks to all-world Russ Francis. Russ was an NFL tight end for the Patriots and 49ers and had won a Super Bowl with San Francisco. So I'm still doing my newsroom "floating" one day— it's a story about a car running a red light with tragic circumstances—the next day, it's a cigar and scotch event at the Kahala. Then Russ enters the picture. First, he's an Oregon guy, played for the Ducks, so I'm immediately friendly, but he rubbed the three guys in the sports cave wrong. They kinda let him hang on his own and he needed some help. He'd come from radio, and the local TV segment had to be much tighter than radio. So after I got done doing whatever I was doing, I'd go help Russ. That was my routine.

Then Russ gets a week-long gig to be involved with the X Games...he was going to be the skydiving or skyflying analyst. Russ goes to the news director and tells him that I am going to do the sports on-air while he's gone. The sports director was like, "Neil's not even in the sports department!" But Russ was a big man and the news director wasn't going to test him, and just like that, I get to do the sports for a week...and I nailed it. At least, that's what most everyone told me. Russ ultimately wound up taking another job, and I was named sports director.

While I was at HPU, we had a basketball player named Brendan Murphy...dude could really shoot the three. We were friends. I wasn't that much older than the athletes I helped tend to. Anyhow, Brendan is in New York City after his HPU days are over...he's working out on a treadmill at some club and strikes up a conversation with a talent agent. Brendan tells him, "You should check out my boy Neil in Hawaii."

So one day I get a call from this guy and he says he wants to represent me. I'm like, "I'm fine right where I am." I LOVED Hawaii...had no plans to move. I was 30-something and groovin'...so I tell this guy, "Get me an interview at ESPN and we'll talk."

He says, "Send me your tape." I did...and figured that was the end of it. Not long afterward, this guy calls me and says, "You got an interview at ESPN."

So I tell him, "I guess you're my agent!"

I get to Bristol and absolutely bomb my audition. The sports I talked about in Hawaii—local high school, surfing, sumo, anything to do with local guys and gals—were way different than ESPN. I should have done my homework, should have prepared better! I thought I was just going to swing in there and everybody was gonna dig me...not how it works. I kicked several names. Called Comiskey Park, "Cominskey Park," could not spit out the name Edwin Encarnacion...it was bad. I was embarrassed! I left believing I had screwed myself and any future I might have had. The thing is, I'd never even thought about working at ESPN...watched Dan Patrick and Keith Olbermann...never thought I'd like to do what they do. I didn't need a dream job; I was already living in my dream state, Hawaii.

So I return to my gig back home...thing is, a lot of folks knew I'd had the audition. Hawaii is small like that...folks, most I'd like to think, were rooting for me...I felt shame having not performed well in Bristol...that's life.

An entire year later, the agent calls me and says, "ESPN wants to give you another audition!" I was floored...he said they saw something they liked. So this time I read the box scores and practiced the names, went back to Bristol and absolutely killed the audition...or so I thought. I was patting myself on the back so much I figured they would hire me before I left town. They didn't. So now I'm back in Hawaii and feeling like I really let Hawaii down...again...I couldn't even watch *SportsCenter* anymore. Started watching CNN sports instead. ESPN was the girl who told me no, and I was kinda heartsick about it.

Then, like three years after that first interview, the agent calls me and says, "ESPN wants to hire you, can you be here in two weeks?"

I said, "I'll be there in two months." Because if I have to leave Hawaii, I'm going out hard. That's what I did!

And it was from there that I got to the position of spending 20-plus years at ESPN. Told you I shouldn't be here...at least not that way!

"Ostrich Races & Rap Music"

-From The Author:

Dari Nowkhah is a massive college sports fan. I'm sure that factored into what was a small leap of faith. Dari left the main ESPN campus after many years as a SportsCenter anchor to take a job with the then-fledgling ESPNU in Charlotte. That faith was rewarded, as Dari has since entrenched himself as the face of the ESPN-owned SEC Network. I can only imagine his excitement at the prospect of his beloved Oklahoma Sooners joining the SEC in 2025.

Dari Nowkhah

·KCFW, Kalispell, MT
·KLKN, Lincoln, NE
·KOTV, Tulsa, OK

·ESPN
·ESPNU
·SEC Network

I earned my degree in broadcast journalism, but that wasn't my original plan. I entered college as a Pre-med major. Then I took chemistry in my first semester. I got a "B" by the grace of the biggest curve upon which I've ever seen a professor grade. I quickly realized I needed to make a change. Pre-med no more, I wanted to be a sportscaster. Three-and-a half-years after changing majors, I walked the stage at the University of Oklahoma with a broadcast journalism degree which, if I was lucky, I *might* put to use in some capacity in the television business.

That was May, 1998. I made my way from Norman, OK to my hometown of Tulsa to live with my parents while trying to land that first TV job. I sent out dozens of resume tapes (yes, actual TAPES back then—no "reels" or email "links") to stations near and far. Meanwhile, I worked as a server at Chili's, a job I had off and on during my college years. I should tell you, I absolutely loved being a server. It's the perfect job for someone who can't sit still for five minutes and enjoys chatting with people. But this was clearly not my ultimate goal. A couple of months went by without so much as a simple confirmation from any news director that my resume and tape had even arrived. So I began training to be a Chili's manager. Yep, I started visualizing my future as a lead "Chilihead."

Then out of nowhere, on a Friday in early August, I got a call. Steve Fetveit was the news director (and station manager and lead anchor) at KCFW-TV, the NBC affiliate in Kalispell, Montana. His was one of 30 or 40 places to which I had sent my material. Steve liked the tape! He told me I was one of 11 candidates he was interviewing for a sports anchor/reporter job. In other words, doing some simple math, I realized I had a 9% chance of landing this job. That is, if he actually talked to all 11. I actually don't think he did, because three days later he called back and asked, "How would you like to come to Montana and work?"

I had never lived outside of Oklahoma. Now I was going to MONTANA?! And not just Montana, but a small town of around 17,000 people tucked away in the northwest corner of the state. The Canadian border was less than an hour away. I had no idea what to expect, but in this crazy business, if any door cracks open, you charge through it.

I jumped into my maroon 1993 Mitsubishi Eclipse and started the drive. Night one, Denver. Night two, Salt Lake City (I loved the Utah Jazz and wanted to see where they played, so I made a detour to SLC). Day three, I pulled into Montana's Flathead Valley, a beautiful place in the northern Rocky Mountains splashed with the bluest lakes I've ever seen. A couple of days later, I settled into my small apartment in Whitefish, a resort town 20 minutes north of Kalispell.

Like most sportscasters, I got into this business to cover Super Bowls, college football championships, World Series, NBA Finals, you get it. But here I was, in an area I had never imagined myself being, covering exactly none of those things. Instead, I spent most of my days at one of four high schools: Flathead, Whitefish, Bigfork and Columbia Falls. And I am forever grateful to the fantastic people I met covering each. I was even grateful on the first Friday of September 1998, when I was enduring a heavy snowfall while filming football games the *first week of the season*. Hey, it's Montana!

Now, let's be honest: I'm in an isolated part of the country, working in small-time television. How would I ever cross paths with someone really famous…like "Shaquille O'Neal famous"? Shaq was, at the time, a megastar with the Los Angeles Lakers. Sure, he would want to come to northwest Montana! Stop laughing. It happened.

A high school basketball official I had gotten to know, Russ, was also a bit of a "promoter." In the summer of 1999, as Shaq was embarking on a rap career, Russ had the rather ambitious idea, "Why not bring him to the Flathead Valley to perform in Kalispell?" Sounds insane, but there was a potential draw here. Legendary NBA coach Phil Jackson is a Montana native and had a home in Lakeside, less than an hour from Kalispell. Jackson, at the time, had just been hired as the Lakers' head coach, so Russ figured maybe Shaq would want to come perform in Kalispell AND get to know his new head coach. Turns out, Russ was right.

A few weeks later, Shaquille O'Neal is in Kalispell, Montana, with a few of his buddies. Even better, Russ put me in touch with him and set up a dinner.

Let me backtrack a bit. As many of you certainly know, when you move away from the only place you've ever known to a place where you know nobody, you need to find friends. I was fortunate. A guy by the name of Mark Opgrande started at KCFW within a week or two of when I did. A native of Longview, Washington, he also knew nobody in Montana. We became fast friends, kept each other out of isolation, and enjoyed countless small-town adventures together. One of which was that unlikely dinner.

The venue was Moose's Saloon, a restaurant/bar in Kalispell—you know, the kind of place you where you chuck your peanut shells on the floor. Not exactly a gathering spot for celebrities. And yet here Mark and I were, with Shaquille O'Neal and his friends, looking at each other thinking, "Are we really dining with Shaq?"

The next day, Shaq "performed" in front of, oh, hundreds (maybe) at the Flathead High School football field. Rap was not exactly popular in this city (in fact, the only FM stations I could find in the area were country music stations, and I have never liked country music). So there was plenty of room for me next to the stage, camera on my shoulder, recording Shaquille O'Neal rapping to a few hundred Montanans. Talk about surreal. And very expensive for "Promoter Russ." I think he might have wished he had that one back.

I had more fun in Montana than I could ever have imagined. But it wasn't just about the Whitefish nightlife! I did have a job to do, and that job offered me a steady string of opportunities for unique "firsts." My weekly features at KCFW included: Learning to ice fish (I was worried about falling in; I never did), learning to snowboard (I caught my front edge all day long), gliding (you have ONE chance to land), and riding in a biplane (we did loopy-loops and one maneuver where the pilot took us completely vertical into the air and then shut off the engine! We plummeted toward the Earth with the engine off before he flipped it back on).

Have you ever heard of ostrich racing? It's a thing, and it happens at the fair in Kalispell. Imagine an L-shaped track.

Racers line up at the end of the short part of the "L," each on the back of a really ticked-off ostrich. The gate opens and immediately, the ostriches try to "shake off" the riders. They spin, jump, hiss, and do anything they can to buck you off. That's when the real fun begins. You win if your ostrich is the first to get to the bend in the track, hang a right and cross the finish line at the top of that "L." So once you're bucked off, you start chasing your ostrich, yelling at it, screaming, hooting and hollering, whatever it takes to get that bird to scoot. You haven't lived until you've seen such an event.

How about furniture races down the side of a mountain? It was an annual tradition at Big Mountain Resort in Whitefish (currently known as the Whitefish Mountain Resort). In early 2000, I had the honor of "judging" a furniture race. The scoring is based on creativity, speed, and accuracy. And by accuracy, I mean…how close do you come to a target at the bottom of the hill without actually hitting it. Yes, you need brakes on your furniture. And yes, you're *on* the furniture as it barrels down the hill. We'd see everything from a couch or a bed on skis to one guy sitting on a toilet with his pants around his ankles as his portable potty rips down the mountain, again, on skis. He nailed the landing, by the way, finishing about a foot from the target before standing up and (mercifully) pulling up his pants.

While summers in the Flathead Valley of Montana are glorious, winters are, um, not so much. I've never been colder than the week before Christmas, 1998. For five straight days, the high temperature was around 30 degrees below zero. The *high* was -30°. One night during that stretch, while walking from the car to a Christmas party with friends, I noticed something happening to my nose, something I had never experienced. I tried to ignore it but could not. Something was terribly wrong inside my nostrils. I looked at a buddy and said, "Dude, something weird is happening inside my nose." He looked at me and said, "You're fine. That's just your nose hairs freezing." Yep, it was cold.

As much as I enjoyed the Montana experience, I did need to advance my career. After almost two years, the time had come to seek a job in a larger market. I had a chance to do that with a job interview in Springfield, Missouri. To be clear, in small- and medium-sized TV markets, stations don't typically spend the money to fly a candidate in for an interview unless they are really serious about that candidate. So I must have done something to screw up my interview, because they didn't hire me.

Thank goodness I did not get that job. Because shortly thereafter, I interviewed at KLKN-TV (ABC affiliate) in Lincoln, Nebraska. I absolutely loved it. And they apparently loved (or at least liked) me. They made me an offer, and I jumped at it. I would miss so much about Montana, but I needed to cover big-time sports to elevate my career. I got that chance with the powerhouse Nebraska football team.

I arrived in April, 2000 and the Huskers were expected to be a top contender for the national championship. They had won titles in 1994, 1995 and 1997 and were basically a machine. I'll never forget Saturdays at Memorial Stadium in Lincoln. The "Tunnel Walk" is one of the most fantastic pregame introduction traditions in college sports. More than 80,000 fans in a sea of red, standing, watching HuskerVision's video on the big screen. The locker room doors fly open, the music blares, the team begins its walk down the tunnel while the camera operator backpedals to keep the shot. The players pause dramatically at the edge of the turf, and then storm out to an eruption of screams and applause. Goosebumps, folks. Goosebumps.

Lincoln is a wonderful city. I made fantastic (and lifelong) friends, of course none more important to me than my now-wife, Jennifer. She was so accepting of my paltry weekend sports anchor salary she paid my way to Cancun after just a couple months of dating! More importantly, she has helped me navigate almost two decades of TV craziness, and for that I am forever grateful.

But it was a low point in Lincoln that I believe allowed me to reach a high level of success in this business. My sports director (main sports anchor) was a man by the name of Matt Kelly. We were good friends and worked well together. We'd routinely produce and host Husker sports specials: football pregame shows, baseball previews, anything that would set our station apart.

Matt worked much harder than I did, which I readily admit now. He would spend seemingly endless time at the station, often into the wee hours of the morning, editing shows, while I went out with friends. I have no idea why I thought that was okay. He and I both hosted the shows, so why wasn't I there in the trenches with him at 2:00 a.m.?

Looking back, I believe I know the answer to that. Like many in this business, I had a pretty healthy ego. Hey, I was 24 years old and on TV! People knew my name when they saw me out and about. I was a celebrity! Thinking about that today makes me want to punch myself in the mouth. But it was my mentality then. Thus, I had a hard time being the "number two" person in our sports department. Even though Matt hired me and I knew my role, I was jealous that he went on all the Husker football road trips, covered the bowl games, etc. I wanted to have those opportunities, but Matt seized them all (as he was completely justified in doing). So, my mindset was, "Hey, you're the big shot here. You take all the trips, you get all of the most fun assignments. It's clearly YOUR sports department, so you can do the late-night work. What do I have to gain by helping?". It was a terribly toxic attitude, but it was how I felt. As my late grandfather Darwin Eaton ("Big Daddy") would have said…"Dar, be careful. You're getting too big for your britches."

One Sunday, I was sitting in our sports office writing my sportscast when Matt walked in. He had just flown back from a Husker road football game, and he wasn't happy. Something was eating at him. Clueless me asked, "What's wrong man, have a crappy flight?" And that was it. Every ounce of Matt's frustration with me came out. Why wasn't I helping him with these shows? Why was I co-hosting the shows but not doing the late-night grunt work? How is that okay? He RIPPED me. By the way, he's about 8 inches taller and could have knocked me through a wall. And briefly, I thought he might do just that. But he made his point. I hated him for a few hours that day, but he was right. We're as close now as we ever were and that story comes up from time to time. That blowup opened my eyes to what it would take to be truly successful in this business.

My stay in Lincoln lasted two years. It was then time to move up again. I needed a larger market. That market happened to be my hometown of Tulsa, Oklahoma. I got a job offer with one month still remaining on my contract in Lincoln. So I bought myself out of that final month for one dollar. Hey, they said I had to "buy myself out" and they named the price. Thank you, Al (you know who you are) for giving me the opportunity to take that next step and leave Lincoln a month early.

Tulsa was…fine. Remember when I said I had a hard time being the "number two" person in the department? At KOTV in Tulsa, I was the number *three*. Numbers one and two were fixtures there at the time, having been in their positions for what seemed like forever. In fact, the sports director, John Holcomb, remains there to this day. Matt Wolfe, the weekend sports anchor, is still one of my close friends. While I was a big fan of both guys, I wasn't afforded the high-profile assignments that would have further advanced my career.

No surprise then, I guess, that the highlight of my tenure in my hometown was not work-related. It was—and is—the highlight of my *life*. May 16, 2003. I married Jenn in Charleston, South Carolina. I have no story that would top that.

Well, except for this. I look back on it now, 17 years later, and can't believe how close I was to never getting to experience working at ESPN. I was *done* with this TV thing. Jenn and I were newlyweds who wanted to start a life together—somewhere. My job was leading me nowhere.

All of us in "local TV" have a decision to make at some point. Do I hire an agent or keep trying to elevate myself in the business on my own? In November, 2003, I hired an agent by the name of Steve Herz. He is based in New York and is the founder and CEO of If Management. Four months later, on a Thursday, Steve called me and asked bluntly, "Can you be in Connecticut on Wednesday?" He had lined up an audition at ESPN. I had an opportunity to land my dream job.

April 1, 2004, was audition day. My day in Bristol was similar to that of just about everybody who has been hired there for an on-air position. You meet a dozen or so executives, sit down with a producer and write a mini-sportscast. Then, go to any one of a dozen studios, sit at the desk, and host that mini-sportscast. Then meet a few more people and leave Connecticut. I was confident I had a good audition. Little did I know what awaited me.

Back in Tulsa, weeks went by. Jenn and I waited desperately for a call from Steve. Either he would say, "ESPN is offering you a job" or "ESPN is going to pass." One way or the other, we needed to know *something*. But regardless of the response, we were finished in Tulsa. We were either moving to Connecticut for the next giant step in my career or to Charleston, SC. Yes, the place we got married. The city in which Jenn had wanted to live since she was a teenager. We said it a hundred times, "Connecticut or Charleston." And if it was Charleston, I was finished with local TV. It had worn me out after six years. We were both planning to become teachers. Sure, we wouldn't make a lot of money. Sure, we were probably headed for a small apartment for who-knows-how-long. But we were ready for it.

How ready? Nine weeks had passed since my audition. Still, nothing from the Worldwide Leader. There was no "we want Dari" or "we're going in a different direction." Nothing. While ESPN didn't seem to have any sort of a deadline on a decision, we did. We let the lease expire on our apartment in Tulsa. Our things were in storage. Jenn had moved back in with her family in Sioux City, Iowa, while I had moved in with my dad, who still lived in my childhood house. In fact, I was staying in my childhood bedroom! We knew we were headed east one way or the other, and figured we would spend a little more time with our families before doing so. "Two weeks," we vowed. "If we don't hear from ESPN in two weeks, we'll tell them we aren't interested anymore and move to Charleston." We had already put down a deposit on an apartment. I was ready to be finished with this TV thing.

A week later, I get the call from Steve. "ESPN is offering you a job."

Connecticut or Charleston? Connecticut won. Jenn gave up her Charleston dream to allow me to live out my ESPN dream. I'll never be able to repay her for that.

I'll say it one more time…this is a crazy business. I've now been with ESPN for 17 incredible years. But I've never grown more, personally and professionally, than I did during those six years in local television.

"A Monkey, A Dog, a Live Shot"

Photo Courtesy: KRTV

-From The Author:

Jaymee Sire and I share a rare bond, having worked on air for both ESPN and NBC Sports (formerly Comcast SportsNet) Bay Area. While I was able to leverage my ESPN experience in getting a job back home in California, Jaymee went the other way, with CSN helping launch her national TV career in Bristol. You can decide for yourself which one of us did it "backward." She is also the inspiration for the "Jaymee Sirewich" at Ike's Sandwiches. Tasty.

Jaymee Sire

·KRTV, Great Falls, MT

·KFMB, San Diego, CA

·Comcast SportsNet Bay Area

·ESPN

·Food Network

I was a high school sophomore in Great Falls, Montana, when I decided on my career path, and I more or less stuck to it. If that sounds ridiculous, well, you haven't met me. When I set my mind to something, there's no turning back. So as a 15-year-old girl who loved the stage—but also enjoyed writing for the school newspaper and yearbook—a television reporter seemed like the perfect mix of all the things I loved to do (and it certainly seemed more attainable than moving to Hollywood to pursue an acting career).

Every decision from that point on revolved around my goal of someday working for a national network. In high school, I ran camera and audio for the local ABC affiliate. It was a split shift and totaled just 2-3 hours a day. I came in for the 5:30 p.m. newscast and returned for the 10:00 p.m. show. It was mind-numbingly easy, but it provided my first glimpse into the glamorous life of local news. The most exciting part was when I forgot to switch the weatherman's camera from TelePrompter to "program" so he could see what he was pointing at on the weather map. He would throw a pen at me to get my attention. But every once in a while, I got to tag along with one of the reporters on my own time and practice my stand-ups, which made the odd hours and terrible pay (and ink marks) worth it.

I chose Washington State University in Pullman for its communications program and got involved with the student-run

TV station, Cable 8, as early on as I could. I took a part-time job running A/V (Audio/Video) for the university. And I got permission to do a summer internship in my hometown after my sophomore year, even though I hadn't started any of my upper-level classes yet. (Don't worry…I wasn't a total book nerd. It was Wazzu after all…one of the Top 10 party schools at the time. It's all about balance!)

To get even more experience, I did a second internship after my junior year at the same station. (By the way, not the one I worked at in high school. But the two shared a parking lot on a hill overlooking Great Falls, because it was the highest point in town, ideal for satellite dish placement). Since this was such a small market (I believe it was TV market 189 at the time, out of 210), they treated me like an extra reporter rather than an intern. I would arrive in the mornings and look on the big white board where all of the assignments for the day were written. Sometimes, I was tasked with simply collecting interviews for a "VO/SOT" (which means "voice over/sound on tape" for the anchor to read). Other times, I would work on a "package," a self-contained story with my voice and multiple sound bites. And every once in a while, I would even get to do a live shot with our one and only satellite truck. I was doing so much work that eventually our news director called me into his office and told me they were going to start paying me. For half my hours…but still! A paid internship in this business was essentially non-existent at the time. For my "real" job, I was a hostess at Applebee's in the evenings. Living the dream.

I still remember my first live shot because it was such a disaster. We didn't have IFB capabilities, which, thinking back is pretty insane (an IFB is the earpiece reporters wear so we can communicate with the control room). Instead, my videographer would be on the phone with the director back at the station. The director would cue the videographer, who would in turn cue me when it was time to speak. I couldn't hear the anchor's lead-in, so everything had to be carefully scripted ahead of time.

The story was at the airport, where vintage planes were going to be on display for a couple of days, and I was set to interview someone about the event. Turns out one of the planes was running late, and for safety reasons we had set up further back than we would've liked. Shortly before my live shot, the plane landed, so my videographer decided to move closer to get a better backdrop. There was a more seasoned reporter with us to help me out, and she was listening to the newscast on AM radio where it was simulcast. She heard the anchor reading my lead-in, so she cued me to start talking. Which I did. Our videographer was still setting up the shot and waved for me to stop. Which I did. He then cued me again, so I started my whole interview over.

As I'm sure you can guess, not only was the entire fiasco broadcast live, but the director took the shot while the camera was still focusing AND zoomed in all the way on my face. I got back to the station, and our sports anchor said to me, "Don't watch it." Of course, I had to, and it was every bit as cringey as it sounds. But I can confidently say it only got better from there!

By the time I graduated college, I had two internships under my belt and felt I was ready for the next step up in television markets. However, during my senior year, I decided to switch my focus from news to sports, and while I had a ton of reporting experience for someone just out of school, my resume "reel" was mostly filled with news stories. Plus, I had studied abroad in Europe for the final semester of my senior year, which meant I couldn't begin the tedious process of mailing out VHS tapes to stations until I returned home from my travels. (Kids these days have it so easy! You literally just send someone a link.)

In the meantime, I started doing fill-in work at the station where I'd spent two summers interning (KRTV, the local CBS affiliate). Soon thereafter, they had an opening for a morning/noon anchor and offered me the job. I didn't really want it, but figured it was better than nothing so I said "yes," as I waited for something better to come along. It was a terrible shift. I arrived at 4:00 a.m., was on air at 6:00 or 6:30, and then again at noon. But I wasn't just the anchor. I was also the producer, which meant I had to create the show from scratch, mostly by repurposing the 10:00 p.m. news from the night before. The only people at the station that early: me, the weather person, the director, and the janitor (Manny), who also made the coffee and ran studio cameras for our show. (He also brought me mangoes and helped me fix a dent in my car...truly a Swiss-army knife of a human, and I adored him immensely). I was making $18,500 a year, which was well below the poverty line. Luckily, I lived at home. I distinctly remember my younger sister making more that summer as a lifeguard. But hey, I was on TV!

About six months in, our weekend sports anchor announced he was leaving for another job. It was my day off and I saw that our news director had already posted the opening on TVJobs.com. I marched in on my off day and asked (perhaps demanded) the job. He said, "We'll miss you on the news side, but I have no doubt you'll be just as successful doing sports. The job is yours."

The sports department was made up of just two people: the sports director and me. We rarely got to use the live truck or have a videographer shoot our highlights and stories. Our coverage area was "Northcentral Montana." Which meant if there was a big track and field meet on the High Line (two hours away), you were driving there yourself, shooting your own highlights, driving back, editing those highlights, and anchoring the 5:30 p.m. and 10:00 p.m. sportscasts, and maybe shooting a couple innings of the White Sox' rookie ball affiliate in between. I can't tell you how many people would jokingly ask, "Where's your cameraman?" when they saw this 5'4" girl lugging the giant camera and tripod from sporting event to event.

"You're looking at her," I'd quip back.

After six months of doing weekend sports (and weekday news reporting), I got a call from KFMB, the CBS affiliate in San Diego, CA. It was market 26 at the time (again, Great Falls was market 189). I had applied on a whim, assuming I was underqualified for the position, but also thinking I might have a slim chance, since the main duties of the gig included reporting on high school football for their new Friday night show (after all, I sort of looked like I was in high school). They wanted to fly me out for an interview! They also asked if I had any additional live shots to show them, so I put together a secondary audition tape with a recent story I had done at the Montana State Fair. And it was quite the story.

There was a woman at the Fair that year who had a show that featured a monkey racing around a track on top of a dog (yes, that's considered news in Montana!). She let me hold the monkey for my live shot and of course, as soon as I began talking, the monkey started climbing all over me. I didn't miss a beat, not even when the cheeky primate grabbed my chest just as I tossed back to studio. The news director in San Diego later told me that live shot was what landed me the job.

That's not to say I wasn't completely underqualified and in way over my head. I probably had no business making that seismic career leap. For about six months, I was convinced the powers-that-be would realize the error of their ways and exercise their "out" after year one of my four-year contract. Thankfully, they saw something in me that suggested I could actually do the job if given the opportunity.

They threw me right into the fire on my second day, sending me to a Padres game to do a live shot. Up until this point, my experience covering professional sports was limited to rookie-level baseball. This was the big leagues, figuratively and literally. Fortunately, I interviewed Mark Loretta that day, who is one of the nicest athletes I've ever covered, and he made it fairly easy on me. The live shot wasn't as disastrous as my first one back in Montana, but it was plenty awkward. Lucky for me, I don't like being bad at things, so I worked my butt off to get better, and they let me stick around for the full four years.

I even got to dip my toe into sideline reporting. At the time, that was my dream—to eventually take over *Monday Night Football* duties. Our station produced and aired the pre-season Chargers games (back when they played in San Diego). One year, they finished the preseason at Candlestick Park in San Francisco. As was typical in San Diego on Labor Day weekend, it was about 75-80 degrees and sunny. Not having yet experienced the pleasure of SF weather, I assumed the same would be true up north. If you've ever visited San Francisco in the summer, you are likely chuckling to yourself already. I showed up in a 3/4 length summery "jacket." I put jacket in quotes because it wasn't really a jacket at all. It was more fashion than function, and I regretted my clothing choice before the game even kicked off.

There is a famous quote (often incorrectly attributed to Mark Twain) that states: "The coldest winter I ever spent was a summer in San Francisco." Truer words were not spoken that night, as I shivered my way through a meaningless pre-season NFL game. The equipment staff took pity on me and gave me a giant, puffy, full-length down coat to wear. At first, I would take it off right before my sideline hits, but by halftime I threw caution to the cold, misty, swirling Candlestick wind and just wore that thing on camera for the rest of the game.

As it turned out, my next career stop took me to the Bay Area so I knew what to expect when I moved there in 2008. I was the first hire at the new Comcast SportsNet Bay Area regional network. We officially launched the network with a full slate of programming in 2009, and in 2010 they assigned me to cover the Giants baseball beat. If you know your baseball history, you know that was a very good time to start covering the team as they went on to win a World Series title that year. The Giants won again in 2012, and added a third championship in 2014 after I left.

People often ask me which sport I prefer to cover and I always say baseball. I think it's because they play every day, so you really get a chance to know the players (for better or worse). Of course, like any female covering a male sport, I had to navigate my way through inappropriate clubhouse comments and Pablo Sandoval hitting me with a shaving cream pie mid-interview with Angel Pagan, but for the most part those teams hold a special place in my heart.

If it were up to me, I would have reported full time. But they didn't have the budget to send me on the road, so I would fill in on the anchor desk when the team was away. I never had aspirations of becoming an anchor, and honestly that probably came across in my work. My news director at the time sat me down in his office and told me I could be one of the best anchors in the country—if I actually tried. That really struck a chord with me, and from there on out, I started putting equal effort into my reporting and anchoring.

As it turns out, I did go on to anchor quite a bit, and at ESPN, no less. Ironically, I helped launch a morning show which, in a way, brought my career full circle. I feel so old now, recounting these stories as I watch girls straight out of college land big-time jobs simply from notoriety on apps like YouTube and TikTok. But honestly, I wouldn't have it any other way. It might sound cheesy, but you really do appreciate both the journey and those who assisted in that journey—the videographers, editors, producers, and makeup artists—so much more when you remember doing all those jobs yourself.

"Put It in a Bag, Boys"

-From The Author:

John Buccigross is an ESPN original. Not to be confused with an original ESPNer—he's not that old—he is simply unlike any other anchor we've seen. Bucci has become a SportsCenter legend over the last quarter-century, thanks to a winning combination of great writing, cleverly subtle catch-phrases, and a dash of quirkiness. Oh, and I should mention that one of my goals in life is to someday win the #Bucciovertimechallenge on Twitter

John Buccigross

·WCVX, Hyannis, MA

·Cape 11 News, MA

·WPRI TV12 Providence

·ESPN

I looked for my first job in television by looking in a phone book. Specifically, the yellow pages. I say that to college students today with their social media accounts and their agents and they come back with two questions: "What's a phone book?" and "What are yellow pages?"

I was a certified hayseed when I graduated from Heidelberg University in 1988. My family didn't come from money, so we didn't travel. Thus I spent a large percentage of my life in my small hometowns in Ohio and Pennsylvania. It was like the colonial 1800s. I didn't have cable TV until I was 12 and the internet was not even fathomable, even though it was only eight years away for most common folk. Worldly? I barely knew what was going on outside my county, except what was on ESPN or MTV. As a result, I didn't have a clue how to even *look* for a job in TV.

"Mom, where's the phone book?!?"

Since my parents moved to Plymouth, Massachusetts, the summer after I graduated from college, that's where the phone book was. Looking under "Television Stations" in the yellow pages, I found a station in Hyannis, on Cape Cod, called WCVX, Channel 58. So I called the station in the spring of 1989 and, after being told there were no jobs, offered to work for free at night. I came to find out the station was bleeding money like a hooked large-mouth bass and was to be dead and dark in two years. To me it looked shiny and big and I figured ABC, NBC, and CBS all looked like that.

I did this while working at a store called Chess King in the local Cape Cod Mall, selling terrible men's clothing. Employees got a stout 40% discount, so my wardrobe in 1989 consisted primarily of terrible Chess King clothing.

My time at Channel 58 in Hyannis must have broken about 14 different labor laws. I worked for free. I never signed any kind of waiver. What if a camera fell on me? But two important things happened there. First, they helped make a resume tape that I could at least show stations, by letting me do a make-believe sportscast in their nice-looking studio as I searched for that first paying job, as it was a now 12 months after graduation. Secondly, sports anchor Bob Halloran, who let me shoot, edit, and write copy he would use on air, told me about a tiny news operation a few miles away in South Yarmouth called *Cape 11 News*. It was where Bob started before he "hit the big time" at the over-the-air Channel 58. Little did he know he was sailing on the television Titanic. Rest easy, Bob's television news career is still going strong in Boston. We would end up being employed simultaneously in Providence, RI, at WPRI-TV12, and later at ESPN.

Cape 11 News was in the same building in which Cape Cod Cablevision customers paid their cable bill. It was like working on the set of *Office Space* with one small 20-by-20-foot TV studio. This was not the big time. Nine people turned out a half-hour local newscast, Monday through Friday. If something happened on Cape Cod over the weekend, it would have to wait until Monday. *Cape 11 News* was essentially a carpeted cable access show; a service for those with cable to add some value to their package.

So in June 1989, at the direction of Bob, I drove 15 minutes over to South Yarmouth and the *Cape 11 News* glorified closet to meet with news director, Martha Cusick, who was the daughter of Boston Bruins Hall of Fame hockey broadcaster, Fred Cusick. I dropped off the resume tape I constructed at Channel 58 after Martha said she had nothing to offer at the time, but would keep me on file.

A few weeks later, Martha called to inform me she had been approved to hire a part time videographer to work from 4:00-10:30 p.m., and that's how my "paying" television career began on August 23rd, 1989.

The duties were to help with the 5:00 p.m. newscast, play the recorded tape of that newscast at 7:00 p.m., be a cameraman for the night reporter (or go solo), and then get back in time to press play on the videotape machine at 10:00 p.m., to replay the newscast again. The way this was done was 1989 going on 1959. An intricate process. At 7:00 p.m. and 10:00 p.m., I would have the newscast cued up, with the play button and pause button both on. But at the same time, I would have to press another button that would allow our control room to overrun the normal *CNN Headline News* channel that was airing on people's TVs at home. Simultaneously hit play on the tape deck and press a hard plastic blue button, and once again Cape Cod had its wall-to-wall carpeting local news studio.

The minimum wage in 1989 was $3.35 an hour. I got a whopping $6.00 an hour, which came out to $7,800 a year. But the important caveat was that when the sports anchor, Bryan Ramona, was off work, I got to fill in. My first sportscast would occur in October, 1989.

A couple months later, the news director was approved to make my job into a 2:00 p.m.-10:30 p.m. full-time gig as videographer/backup sports anchor as of New Year's Day, 1990. The job paid $15,000 a year. I celebrated by purchasing a 1987 Nissan Maxima for $10,500 with an interest rate of about 94%. I still had no idea how life worked. I also got engaged to my very attractive, way out of my league girlfriend, Melissa Monroe that May. I bought an engagement ring at Kay Jewelers in early 1990 for $5,200. So, between the Maxima and the ring, I had essentially "spent" my entire $15,000 salary. Certified idiot.

Unexpectedly, Bryan Ramona moved on from the sports director job in April, 1990 and I was able to pivot to full-time sports guy. I got a $3,000 raise—to $18,000—and my salary would remain at that level for the next four-plus years, through a wedding Melissa and I had to pay for, two kids, and two burned out clutches on the Nissan Maxima. I should mention I bought the Maxima, a 5-speed, DESPITE NOT KNOWING HOW TO DRIVE A STANDARD. I learned on the fly and paid the price in maintenance. I would put 250,000 miles on it and sell it for $500 in 1996.

Thankfully, this initial paying TV job of mine was pre-internet. The 1990s, especially the early 90s, were the last great decade of mankind. The final precious years before widespread internet and cell phones. The world was slower, more personal, and you could suck on television and make some mistakes without everyone seeing it on a loop via social media. It was also a time of "old school" office rules. For instance, the cable TV portion of the building was always celebrating something: Christmas, a good year of subscriptions, something. The beer and wine were flowing around the cubicles and offices at, like, five in the afternoon.

With that in mind, it at least became *plausible* that one could enjoy a beer at this particular workplace. Right? Well, once upon a time, another young up-and-comer, Doug Meehan, who has enjoyed a long career anchoring morning shows across the country, and I were ready to go out on a Friday night. But first we had to press play and rerun our newscast at 10:00 p.m. We thought we would get a head start on the evening and bought a couple of beers at the package store across the street. We went into the control room, pressed play to start the repeat of the newscast, literally put our feet up, and cracked open a beer. I mean, it was Friday night. The building was empty except for the 24-hour cable dispatcher in the back.

So there we are, feet up, counting down the minutes until we could hit a summer night on Cape Cod, sipping our Old Milwaukee Light and shooting the breeze…when in walks the general manager of this branch of Cape Cod Cablevision, Gerry Buckley. He was a big man with a big head and a thick Boston accent. We are screwed. I got a wife, a kid, I make $18,000 a year, and my life and career are passing before my eyes.

With our hearts in our stomachs, Buckley looks at me and Doug and says matter-of-factly, "Put it in a bag, boys," and walks out.

GOD BLESS AMERICA.

Yes, the confluence of "the times," youth, and a complete lack of options conspired to make my first job into a delicate balance of working every day for my livelihood, while making wildly terrible decisions like cracking open a beer before punching out at work. Another time, we didn't have a car available for a Friday night out so we took the news van to a Cape Cod nightclub/bar. I mean, why not?

We worked hard and played hard. We were young and poor, but full of life and optimism. I think there was a recession going on, but this new adult world still seemed pretty cool. The world—and news operations—weren't so political. There was no social media; there were no selfies. Oh, and I still had no idea how I would get my next job.

Thankfully, I survived the first one. I stayed for more than five years. Most people get burned out after a couple, then look to make the next step to a city like Charleston, South Carolina, or Manchester, New Hampshire. I enjoyed Cape Cod so much I wanted to skip that step and be patient while enjoying my young family on the Cape, 30 minutes away from my parents. Luckily it worked out, as I moved on to Providence, Rhode Island, in 1994. I was 28. It was the 44th largest market at the time and it gave me the chance to cover professional sports teams like the Red Sox, Patriots, Celtics, and Bruins. Two short years later, I was hired at ESPN, which had been my dream all along.

There are no news vans at ESPN and I've never had a beer inside the building. But my journey shows it's not necessarily who you know or where you started that matters most. It's how you finish. And above all, when in doubt, "put it in a bag."

"The Midnight Search for a Suit"

Photo Courtesy: Albuquerque Journal

-From The Author:

Andy Katz is carrying the flag, so to speak, as the lone "TV guy" among our cadre of 'casters that initially reached the national stage as a "print guy." Rest assured, that transition is not an easy one. Andy's journey from newspaper reporter to high-profile TV analyst is emblematic of how the business has evolved over the last couple of decades. It also earned him some quality time with then-President Barack Obama. Who knew NCAA "brackets" could be such the ticket to greatness?

Andy Katz

·WIBA-AM, Madison, WI   ·ESPN
·Milwaukee Journal Sentinel   ·Turner Sports
·Albuquerque Journal   ·Big 10 Network
·Fresno Bee   ·FOX Sports

The path doesn't seem to be as straight today as it was 30 years ago.

That's the way it should be.

Journalism should evolve. But one thing remains clear: To get to your dream job, the obstacles are many and how you handle/hurdle them will determine your fate.

This is just one snapshot of my story.

Day one at the University of Wisconsin. I walked into the *Daily Cardinal* office, ready to work, willing to do anything. And that meant taking on the sports that didn't get the headlines. I loved it. I covered women's soccer as well as the more "high-profile" men's basketball and football. There was a hierarchy, and you had to prove that you were willing to learn how to report and cover a team to earn your way.

The beauty of working at the *Daily Cardinal* in Madison was how much I learned about life, culture, and the decisions to live as you see fit. Love who you want, live and dress in a style that fits you. Without judgment.

I'll never forget when I was the sports editor—the youngest ever at the time as a sophomore—and our photographer had an assignment to shoot a day in the life of the school. He returned with pictures of only white students. He hadn't ventured to Union South where there were more Asian students. He hadn't found any Black students. He was sent

115

back out. The photographer was told to show the whole campus, not just the assumed perception of a Wisconsin student. I love that he was pushed back out there to assemble a more accurate depiction.

I wore many hats during my college years. I worked for WIBA radio, gathering sound at Packers and Brewers games. I took high school stats at the *Wisconsin State Journal*. But my break came as a senior when I had the opportunity to be the student paid intern at the *Milwaukee Journal*. That entailed backing up the full-time person, who lived in Madison. He would cover men's basketball and football. I would do hockey and any other stories that were warranted. I lucked out with the hockey team, which won the national title and got me front-page stories. But it was a random assignment that would ultimately change my career and, in a way, my personal life.

Aaron Pryor, a boxer, was making a comeback in Madison. I had no passion for boxing. I had never covered the sport. I grew up in the Boston area, so I knew about Marvin Hagler. Of course, I followed Muhammad Ali. But Pryor was an unknown to me. I immersed myself in the story, went to his workouts, made sure I was "all-in" on his comeback from an eye injury, and then covered the fight, which he won. The stories got front-page placement.

I was heading toward full-time status at the *Journal*. The catch was, the job's availability hinged on the Milwaukee Admirals becoming an NHL expansion team. I was in line to be the beat writer, a promise I had from Chuck Salituro, the sports editor at the time, as well as my future ESPN colleague and neighbor in West Hartford, Connecticut. Unfortunately, the

Chicago Blackhawks blocked the expansion deal, and that full-time job never materialized.

So I had to cast a wide net to find work. I applied all over the country, constantly scouring *Editor and Publisher* magazine looking for job openings. I was frustrated and not sure I would ever get a full-time gig. So much so I even paid a visit to the Naval recruiting office. I was a history/poli-sci major with a minor in Soviet and East European Studies. I had done a James Bond-like trip in 1986, bringing Jewish religious items to Refusniks, who were Jews in exile in the former Soviet Union. I had visions of being a spy.

When I put together my resume for the *Albuquerque Journal*, I decided to include the Aaron Pryor clips. Why not? What I didn't know was that the sports editor at the time, Mike Hall, was a huge boxing fan. Albuquerque happens to have a long boxing history. The clips of Pryor stood out, even though I was applying to cover the University of New Mexico men's basketball team. Mike would later tell me those boxing clips were the clincher. Diversity of coverage ended up being a major plus.

I went for an interview in June. I had never been to New Mexico. I *had* eaten spicy Mexican food. So it wasn't surprising that (in my dark suit, knit tie, and suspenders) I sweated profusely during the interview at a local joint called Los Cuetas.

After the interview, I had time to kill, so I decided to go to the movies. I left the car running as I ran up to the theater to check the movie times. Then, in my haste to get back to my running car, I slammed the side of my head into a pole. I had a ringing headache and did not realize until later I had given myself a concussion. I flew home and ended up on three days of bed rest after the clumsy incident.

Weeks later, while on a post-graduation trip to Alaska, I got out of Denali National Park to call home. My father told me Hall had called. I called him back and he offered me the job. I took it. Two years later, I would meet my wife Denise in Albuquerque and we now have two wonderful children, Lucia and Salvador.

But that makes it sound as if it were smooth sailing up to the time I met Denise in the spring of 1991. It wasn't.

This was my first job out of college. I had never lived in the Southwest. I was actually taking the beat job of a much older, longtime writer at the *Journal*. He wasn't happy about it at all, and most certainly didn't appreciate that they promoted my arrival with an over-the-top ad campaign—me dressed in a tux, converse around my neck, shades and a basketball.

And while Hall gave me the job, loved my boxing coverage, and had faith in me, he didn't do me any favors in the beginning.

Covering UNM basketball was akin to covering Indiana, Kentucky, and Kansas within the state. It was a big deal. Hall didn't want to take the previous writer off the beat entirely, so he sent him with me. On the road. In the same room (yes, there was a time when reporters had to room together to save money).

He was probably 20 years older than I was. And this was 1990-91, when the economy was getting tight. He knew his job was on the line. So on the road, late at night in the room, he would work on me, trying to get me to leave. The lights would be out and he would tell me that I had to have come from

118

money—since I was Jewish and from the East Coast. That, of course, wasn't true and just an anti-Semitic stereotype. We were middle class. My father was a law professor at Boston College. My mother was a clinical social worker for the state of Massachusetts. We were fine. We weren't rich. I wasn't given any kind of allowance or trust. I was in New Mexico on my own and had to earn everything I got.

But the former writer worked on me every night on the road. I would actually hide under the covers in the adjoining bed, trying to ignore his drivel.

Finally, a breaking point. I confronted Mike Hall and said if I'm going to cover the team, I need to have a different roommate or a single room. He obliged, and I ended up rooming with our staff photographer.

I left Albuquerque in 1995 for a job with the *Fresno Bee*. But it's the story of my arrival at ESPN that I believe best demonstrates the lengths to which you sometimes must go to prove your journalistic skills.

It was Labor Day weekend in 1999. I flew from San Francisco to Hartford (yes, there was a direct flight on United back then). Remember, this was pre-9/11, which is key. I had a small carry-on and my suit in a sleeve, which I had asked to store in the first-class closet. I was sitting in coach. When we arrived, I walked to the front to look for my suit. It was gone. Someone had taken it, I assume by mistake.

I ran through the airport, flipping back suit sleeves people were carrying, thinking they might be mine. No luck. I went to the United baggage area and saw a suit hanging behind the worker at the desk. It was a tux, not mine. Hold that thought.

I was at a loss. I had an interview with ESPN.com and ESPN TV at 9 a.m. John Marvel from ESPN.com was going to pick me up at the hotel in Bristol at 8:00 a.m. for breakfast. I was wearing a T-shirt and jeans. Clearly I couldn't show up like that—I was interviewing to be *the* college basketball reporter for the network! At the time, the only other sport-specific reporters there were Chris Mortensen and John Clayton for the NFL, David Aldridge for the NBA, and Peter Gammons for Major League Baseball. That's it. This was a big interview.

I had no suit. I ran back to the United desk. I asked the guy there if he could tell me where the flight attendants stay. He gave me the hotel info (no way that happens now!). I called and actually got one of the flight attendants on the phone. I told her about my plight and the tux. She recalled a person in first class who was heading to a wedding. She gave me his name. I called information in San Francisco, got his number and left a message, hoping he would retrieve his messages remotely.

I went back to the United desk and asked the guy if I could try on the tux to see if it would fit, thinking at least showing up in a tux would make for a good story. He wouldn't allow it.

I called my dad to see if he could drive down from Newton to Bristol with clothes. But he's shorter than I am. Nothing he had would fit. And I had no clothes at their house anymore.

I asked if there was anything open at 10:00 p.m. Turns out there is a Walmart somewhere near the Farmington Valley. I call. I have the worker walk up and down the aisle. He has pants. A shirt. No jackets and no ties. No go. My wife, to whom I've been talking on the phone—a pay phone, mind you—tells me there is a mall. The Westfarms Mall. But it doesn't open until 10:00 a.m., which is too late.

I'm upset. I'm at a loss. I kick a trash can. Suddenly, a state trooper arrives, telling me I have just damaged federal property. He takes my license and I hear him read my name as it echoes across other radios among the troopers in the building. I have no record. I'm told to leave. The rental car company is closing. I have to get my car and drive to Bristol. It's after midnight.

While driving, I turn on ESPN Radio. I lived on the West Coast and had been a frequent guest on their late-night show, which give me an idea. One final "Hail Mary." I call the show's producer, Louise. I tell her my story. I ask—really, *beg*— whether anyone on the campus is my size. She tells me to hold on. Jay Reynolds gets on the phone. He's the overnight update reporter. He tells me he thinks he has a suit for me, but I'd have to meet him when he gets off work and follow him to Simsbury where he was living with his mother.

I tell him I will. I don't sleep. I meet Jay at 5:00 a.m., then follow him through the dark, winding roads of rural Connecticut. We get to his house. His mother, a teacher, was up getting ready. She makes us breakfast and irons my shirt. I leave and make it back to Bristol, shower, and change before Marvel picks me up for the day.

I go through the "car-wash" of interviews, including one with Bob Eaton, who tells me that he can't promise I'll ever get on television. I go out to eat later that night in Bristol and find out that I'm likely going to get the job. I do, and wind up spending 18 years at ESPN.

The lesson? Persistence. Never stop trying to get the job done. And never stop using your reporting skills—even when it's just to get a suit for an interview.

"Lady Luck's Twinkling Glance"

-From The Author:

Kevin Corke is the epitome of TV overachievement. I'm fairly certain he is the only person in history who has anchored at ESPN, NBC News, and FOX News...and worked as a coordinating producer at ESPN...and earned two master's degrees, including one from Harvard. So it should come as no surprise that he is currently enrolled in law school. Because, apparently, you can never have too much education. And to top it all off, "Corkie," as we call him, can rock a bow tie like few others.

Kevin Corke

·KRDO, Colorado Springs, CO   ·NBC News
·KUSA, Denver, CO   ·FOX News
·ESPN

It was a little before 3:00 a.m. on a brisk southern Colorado Saturday morning. A crystal-clear, starlit night, and nearing the conclusion of a very long week of editing work at KRDO-TV in Colorado Springs. A fall chill hung in the air that night, not quite cold enough for a down-filled winter coat, but I wore one anyway.

Then, just as suddenly as a deer hops into traffic, stares, then sprints across the road, there was a tap on the driver's side window of my car. Not the kind that gently awakens you from a restful slumber. Rather, a jolt-inducing rap instigated by a heavy-duty Maglite flashlight.

Tap, tap, tap…"Sir, are you ok?" asked the surprisingly young security guard, holding that wicked, bright light close to his ear.

"Fine, fine, thanks," I said, squinting, groggy, yet keenly aware of how precarious such interactions can be. "Just getting a little shut-eye. Long week," I added.

"Well, there's a lounge inside for families if you want," offered the guard, now turning to walk away. I said thanks, he said no problem and that was that.

Alas, my surprisingly uncomfortable, overnight snore-fest in the front seat of my silver, 1978 Honda Civic had come to an end. I spent the next couple of hours listening to AM radio (some guy named Art Bell, talking about UFOs), then drove off to a nearby McDonalds where I promptly washed up and ordered a couple of breakfast sandwiches and a Coke.

I'd spent that night in a hospital parking lot. I figured it would be safer for a young African-American than just chillin' in my car on some random neighborhood street overnight...to say nothing of professionally wiser than admitting to my new colleagues at Channel 13 that I actually didn't have a place to sleep that night, or the money to rent a room at the nearby Motel 6, which at the time cost less than $30. Mind you, on a $4.05 hourly salary, Ramen noodles were a staple and occasional sub sandwiches were a treat, so booking a motel wasn't, shall we say, in the cards.

Why was I without lodging that particular night? Well, my new roommate at the time (and co-worker for all of four weeks) was hosting his girlfriend for the weekend. I'd agreed to "get lost," figuring I would head to my sister's home in Denver. But when my alternate lodging plan suddenly changed (er, um, another sleepover?), I resigned myself to the car. Which was fine, because Denver was 75 miles away. Had I left town, I likely would not have made it back for what turned out to be a very busy, and very important, sixth day of work that week. Plus, the extra work day meant another $32.80 (before taxes) in my pocket. Trust me, when you're driving a car you bought used for $150, an extra $20 for gas goes a long way.

My job at the time entailed primarily editing, but since I began my career as a photographer at KRDO's "southern" bureau in Pueblo, I was sometimes called upon to pick up a camera pack (more about that later) and help shoot high school sports. That particular day, I'd planned to help edit footage from a couple of prep football games, then shoot a portion of a local cycling race, *where I would get to record an on-camera standup*—a rare and golden opportunity!

My dream had always been to be an on-air reporter, but getting my foot in the door in the TV business meant shooting and editing…so of course, I went for it. As is often the case in small markets, at KRDO there was lots of jockeying to get your face on television. People would work early, late, and on off-days for the opportunity to shoot their own stories and offer them to weekend producers, with the hope of sneaking one on air without the news director's knowledge (and potential objection). This cycling story was my chance. But had I not been there that morning, that piece could have gone to any number of other reporters or interns who were clamoring for a little face time. I would have missed out on shooting that standup, which wound up being instrumental in helping me get my first on-air job 18 months later.

Now, one could argue that sleeping in my car in town instead of driving to Denver that night was a case of blind and/or dumb luck…and you'd be on solid footing to do so. But upon further reflection, I've come to believe that, particularly early in my career, I was a frequent recipient of Lady Lucky's twinkling glance. For me, plain old good fortune—dumb luck, if you prefer—was as big a contributor to my early success as hard work, perseverance, and all that cliché kinda stuff. Truly!

As the ninth of ten children, I grew up immersed in—and fascinated by—sports. I had one brother invited to a minor league baseball camp and another who played major college football. I grew up on Pop Warner and a steady dose of street Wiffle ball, and later played *four* sports in high school: wrestling, football, tennis, and track. With that family history—combined with years of binge-watching any and all varieties of sporting events, boxing matches, Olympics, etc.—it's not surprising that I always wanted to become a sportscaster. "This is Howard Cosell," I'd say often, mimicking the legendary broadcaster.

When you're the ninth of ten kids in a family, you learn four things quickly:

1) You'll never ride in the front seat of the car
2) You'll never pick what's on TV
3) Nothing you wear will be new
4) When to keep your mouth shut

All jokes aside, one of the most unique things about my early career in television was the fact that as the first child in my family to graduate from college, I felt a deep sense of responsibility (an obligation really) to give a damn. To give an honest day's work and always try to do the right thing, whether the boss was watching or not.

Exhibit A: the very first story I covered, back when I was a photographer at the KRDO Pueblo bureau. A reporter and I were sent to a "grow house" which had been raided by local police. Picture a large barn. On the outside, it looked like any other barn you'd see in this rural part of the state. But inside, it's wallpapered from floor to ceiling with aluminum foil. And of course, there were rows of marijuana plants. Dozens of them, most more than eight feet tall. All of this was illuminated by obnoxiously bright lights which emanated from the ceiling and reflected off of the wall-to-wall foil. It was the kind of thing you'd expect to see in a movie, but for me it was simply day one on the job.

I hastily shot video all over the house, and then, since there was no police tape restricting my movement, went into the basement for additional footage. Once downstairs, my eyes were drawn immediately to a table covered in $100 bills. There must have been $15,000 on that table and the floor nearby, as if someone had taken a pillowcase and just dumped it. Would anyone have noticed if a couple bills suddenly "disappeared?" That didn't matter because of my disposition to do the right thing. I then noticed at least a dozen weapons, including what appeared to be a pair of old M1903 rifles, along with boxes and boxes of ammunition.

My reporter, Ken, had asked me to look for unusual camera shots, so I opened the refrigerator to take some video. Inside I saw flour tortillas and butter, and literally nothing else. No milk, no water, nothing. That is, until I opened the freezer to find foil packs resembling small bricks. I wasn't sure exactly what they were, but I suspected they were not legal. So I shot those, too, which made my reporter's day. And mine.

I drove home that night in my gas-starved Civic. (The tank was always somewhere between a quarter-full and empty). But I didn't care about running on fumes. I was running on adrenaline, basking in the exhilaration of the day. And remembering how thankful I was just to be working in this crazy business.

That said, one thing I will never miss about being a cameraman is the photography pack I had to schlep around with me. Those packs included the camera (not exactly a light lift in those days), the adjoining videotape deck (connected by coax cable), a sizeable Sachtler tripod, light belt, sunlamp, battery packs, and other assorted accoutrement needed to tell stories out in the field. Necessary tools of the trade at the time, and considerably larger and heavier than today's fare.

To stay nimble, I didn't always carry the entire pack with me (especially on sports shoots). When the action is coming your way, ease of mobility is key. So I usually carried a camera, deck, batteries...and that was it. While the main station in Colorado Springs didn't often need high school football or basketball footage from Pueblo for our Friday night prep sports extravaganza, sometimes such duty called.

On one occasion, I found myself shooting a football game in the late afternoon hours. The skies to our west were iron gray, and I knew a storm was moving in (as is fairly common in Colorado on hot summer days). I wanted to get just a couple of touchdowns recorded, hop in my car, and drive to the bureau to feed the videotape (via microwave) to the main station. I'm not sure how much we knew about Doppler in those days, but I do know I didn't expect what happened next.

I was standing around the 30-yard line with game action heading my way from the opposite 30-yard line. Without warning, just as a play ended, there was a blast of bright light that zapped a tree about 20 yards past the end zone to my right. It sent the leaves at the top of the tree fluttering down like someone had taken a feather-filled pillow and swung it violently until all the feathers flew out of it. Smaller branches fell to the ground and there was a noticeable scar where lightning had struck the tree. Fortunately, no one was hurt and there were no stands for fans over there...but the bolt ended the action on the field and sent everyone scrambling to their cars or indoors. I didn't know enough to *not* be standing out there carrying all that gear while electricity was dancing about the heavens. But I can tell you, to this very day, if there's inclement weather in the area, I'm out. Period. Full stop. My hair is curly enough.

During my time in the Pueblo bureau, I worked with a prince of a man by the name of Ken Moon. He hosted a weekend radio show which primarily focused on real estate, but he did get a chance to do a bit of TV on the side—likely owing to his relationship with key, high-level station management figures. Sounds funny now, but when you think about it, Ken was actually pretty shrewd. You can pick up some pretty decent coin selling houses, and who doesn't want to buy real estate from the local TV guy? Ken managed to keep a foot in both worlds—along with his radio hustle—but always made time for me, answering questions about life and, of course, about how to progress in the TV business.

With Ken's encouragement, I quickly moved upstate from Pueblo to the main station in Colorado Springs to become KRDO's de-facto chief editor, a title I basically gave myself since I was the *only* full-time staff editor (back then, photographers edited their own stories, with rare exception). The move meant working inside the building instead of having to brave the outside elements every day. (Hello, Colorado winters!). And no more schlepping heavy camera gear!

One of the most valuable lessons I learned in that new role was the importance of maintaining professional discretion and source confidence. You might think that as an editor, such a skill set wouldn't be so critical since, generally speaking, editors aren't out in the field collecting stories or working sources.

However, I'd argue that being an editor is akin to being the eyes and ears of the newsroom. Truly it is one of the most intriguing aspects of the job. I not only learned the strengths of some of the great storytellers in the country while in the booth (like renowned iPhone reporter Mike Castellucci), I also learned a great deal about the trials and triumphs of those around me. Over the years, I would help edit countless pieces and 'escape reels' for co-workers, while keeping mum for obvious reasons. The trust others place in an editor is a unique one that I took very seriously. It helped shape not only how I saw the early stages of my career, but how I see it now.

Anyway, remember that Saturday I'd slept in my car? The standup I shot in the field that day? It remained the only actual on-air report I had to put on my resume tape. But thanks to my developing editing skills, combined with my ability to measure and lockdown a tripod and memorize a few lines, I'd go on to make dozens of 'sample reports' which would give me enough material to complete that tape.

Behind it all was a quirky operations manager named Dave Blanco. At 6 feet, 7 inches tall with a long, curly rocker-style haircut, he was more metal than man. Standing next to him, we looked a bit like Danny DeVito and Arnold Schwarzenegger in the movie *Twins*. And like the characters in the film, we made a uniquely successful pairing.

Between commercials, Dave would record my voice tracks. I'd read scripts over and over and then cherry-pick the best segments to cover with video and edit together. We'd laugh at my inability to say the word 'susceptible' and he'd keep my spirits high with encouragement and what might best be described as 'dad humor,' which is to say, pun-heavy and light…safe enough for Ned Flanders to tell.

Thanks to Dave's help, I eventually landed my first full-time on-air job about a year and a half later as sports reporter at KUSA-TV in Denver. And yes, I drove that Honda Civic until it had about 160,000 miles on it, and I've never forgotten how both helped shape my early television career.

KUSA was my dream-come-true, working as an on-air sports reporter in a fantastic sports city. I covered Olympic games, Super Bowls, Stanley Cup Finals, an MLB All-Star game, NBA playoffs, NCAA basketball and football games—including a National Championship—plus major events in golf, cycling, motor sports and tennis. I interviewed countless sports luminaries from Michael Jordan and Tiger Woods to Arnold Schwarzenegger (cheering on Austria's skiers at the World Alpine Ski Championships at Vail) and of course, John Elway.

But few experiences touched me as deeply as my venture to the Indianapolis Motor Speedway in 1991. Photographer Jeff Wilkins and I were there to get a bit of footage ahead of our station's locally produced special on what was then known as the Texaco/Havoline Denver Grand Prix. The Denver race was set for August, but we traveled to the Hoosier state in May to get footage of the Indy 500 to help bolster our Race Day special with some added visual appeal. And just days before the most important race in sports, I had the tremendous honor of interviewing the venerable Mario Andretti.

I told him how my brother, James, had been to the 1971 race won by Al Unser Sr., and managed to bring me back some STP (motor oil) stickers. Gotta tell ya, as a little five-year-old, I was pumped to get those stickers! Mr. Andretti listened politely to my story and after some well-rehearsed sound bites about the beauty of the race at the old Brickyard and the promise of building a tradition in Denver, he looked me straight in the eye and said, "I can see in your eyes you love this sport. Good. Very good."

I replied (my voice a few octaves higher than normal), "I do, I really do."

My photographer, who had (and probably still has) an impish sense of humor, said quietly, "Need to change your shorts, buddy boy?" The timing and the humor itself left a huge smile on my bespectacled face. Though not nearly as much as what would come next.

We were escorted to the track itself and allowed to take three laps for file footage! With Jeff standing and shooting through the sunroof, I drove around the track in a light rain. The camera got soaked and Uncle Wilkie, as he was known, did his best to shoot straight while standing awkwardly on a car seat being driven around a track at 70 miles per hour. I spent those laps looking like Rodney Allen Rippy after a bite of a Jack in the Box hamburger…totally content.

Before we left the Speedway that day, I got out of the car and kissed the bricks on the track. My photographer did too. Somehow, it just seemed like the right thing to do. Because we'd both won a race that day. One of life's many small victories…and an unforgettable one at that. Years later, after I'd made my way to ESPN, watching the Indy 500 had a whole new meaning for me. It was much more than laps around a track. It was a reminder of the road I'd traveled to get to Bristol, and to *SportsCenter*. A road that one day would lead me to covering the White House.

I spent that year working hard to prove I belonged in the 'big leagues." After all, it was a mere two years prior that I was sleeping in my car in Colorado Springs, just hoping for a chance to shoot some games and, someday, get my big break. Someday arrived much sooner than I could have expected. As the old saying goes, "It is what it is, but it will become what you make of it."

I still think about that night back in the hospital parking lot. What if that security guard had given me the 'bum's rush?' Might I have gotten upset and just gone up to Denver that night? What if I had just blown off that weekend and let someone else shoot, edit and submit the stand-up for that special? No one knows for sure how that would have affected my life, but I know this…sometimes it's a tap on the shoulder, and sometimes it's a tap on the driver's side window. But no matter where or when it happens, it's how you respond that can really set into motion a life you only dreamed of.

"The Snow Stopped in Scranton"

Photo Courtesy: Cornell Sun

-From The Author:

Bill Pidto is the most popular anchor in ESPN history—internally. He was the unofficial "Mayor" of Bristol. After Billy's final show in 2008, he walked off the set and received a standing ovation in the newsroom. His "going away" party was the social event of the season, complete with a 20-minute video tribute. He's also likely the only sports anchor known for his catch phrases off-air as much as on-air. To this day, you'll hear references on SportsCenter to a "developing situation" and "black ice," as well as the anticipatory inquiry, "Whadd-u-have?" All Pidto-isms.

Bill Pidto

·WVBR-FM, Ithaca, NY   ·New England Cable News

·CableNewsCenter 7, Ithaca   ·ESPN

·WBNG, Binghamton, NY   ·Mad Dog Radio

·WSTM, Syracuse, NY   ·MSG Network

·Mizlou Sports News Network

Here is the thing. If you complete medical school, you are a doctor, and you can make a great living anywhere. Same goes for someone who finishes law school. Or has an engineering degree. Really, someone in just about any career. Such is not the case for those that aspire to have on-air TV careers. There is no degree that will ensure success. No college that will ensure success. No definitive path that will ensure success. What is worse, everyone wants the same jobs for economic reasons—either in a major media market, or on a major cable network, or on a broadcast network—so all those career lanes inevitably merge. Simply put, you can't make much of a living working in a small market. And because there are no distinct criteria for entry, and because the hiring process is totally subjective, the result is a hyper-competitive career pursuit that is not for the faint of heart.

This is the challenging backdrop for most of us, but my personal situation made it even more so. I was a student at Cornell University, where my peers were headed to law school or medical school or Wall Street. I had an advisor tell me, "You don't want to be on the air, you want to be the person that owns the television station or the person that runs the television station." Even my dad did not completely embrace my career choice.

I remember an article in *Sports Illustrated* during my freshman year profiling the acclaimed Newhouse School at Syracuse University. It predicted that then-senior Greg Papa would be the next "star" to come out of the program (and he did become a star in the Bay Area). There were just so many clues that my elite Ivy League university was somehow the wrong school for what I wanted to do with my life.

But I did get valuable experience on the student radio station, doing sportscasts and working as a color commentator on Cornell football and basketball broadcasts. I then got a big break when a station in the city of Ithaca started a local TV newscast prior to my senior year. I called the general manager week after week prior to the station's opening, until he relented and hired me as one of the original sportscasters, along with Karl Ravech, who went to nearby Ithaca College. For me, this was critical, because I had nowhere else to get television experience or even make a resume tape, which was necessary to apply for other jobs.

Prior to my graduation in 1987, I called every on-air Cornell alum I could track down. The advice I got is the advice I give to this day, which is to say there is no advice except, "Just get on the air!" So I mailed out as many resume tapes as I could and as luck would have it, the CBS affiliate in Binghamton, New York, needed a weekend sportscaster. I made sense as a candidate because I had local experience—Ithaca is 60 miles from Binghamton. But it was only a weekend job, and the news director said he didn't "see a Cornell grad pumping gas to make ends meet," so initially I didn't get the position. Thankfully, a full-time position opened up shortly thereafter, and I was hired as a weekend sports anchor and weekday news reporter. The pay was six dollars an hour. Two of my roommates at Cornell were going to medical school and two had high-paying jobs on Wall Street; I was thrilled just to be employed in television.

I went right from commencement to Binghamton and my parents helped me move into 103 Mason Avenue, where I roomed with two other station employees. The rent? $120 a month. Six bucks an hour salary, about $12k a year, $120 a month rent...I have long joked that I've never had as much disposable income.

103 Mason Avenue basically had no furniture. The rug in the living room was ripped. The refrigerator was empty. A futon and bookcase hardly filled up my bedroom or made it feel like anything resembling home. I will never forget the unease that enveloped me as I was moving in, or the reaction of my mom when she and my dad were ready to leave. I don't think she could believe that *this* was where her son was going to live—in this house, in this unknown, small city, with complete strangers. She literally had tears streaming down her face. We embraced tightly, which for me was as much out of fear as it was love. In what other career, except for a minor league baseball player perhaps, does one start out like this?

Yes, the personal aspect of all this is challenging, but so is the professional life in small market television. Newsrooms are comprised of young, ambitious people—whose primary goal is to move onto greener pastures as quickly as possible—and older, grizzled veterans who are bitter about *not* having moved on. So basically, no one wants to be there. And the embittered veterans are often resentful of the young folks who do have the potential for upward mobility. Our weatherman, near retirement and a local fixture for decades, sat back with us in the sports office and chain-smoked while he watched every single pitch of every Mets game, swearing about every bad development. Our main anchor was miserable and always joked that his stomach hurt the minute he arrived at work. Our lead news producer was obese and inhaled junk food every night. I worked under our main sports anchor, who had been there for years and had wanted out long ago. Again, the economics. It's very hard at that level to do well financially.

But I loved it, even though putting together a sportscast was all-consuming. In a market like Binghamton, reporters had to shoot their own video. Because of the huge emphasis on local high schools and minor league teams, much of my workday was spent with a camera over one shoulder and a huge tape deck over the other. I was a terrible shooter. My basketball video often looked like the game was played on an uneven court. And hockey? The Hartford Whalers and Washington Capitals shared an AHL team in Binghamton, so I had to shoot their games for highlights. It was really hard to follow the puck. Even "white balancing" the camera was a skill I never mastered, so the ice in my video would frequently appear blue.

A typical night would begin with shooting the AHL game for a goal or two, then, depending on the season, it was on to a high school football or basketball game (or two). Then it was back to the station to edit the highlights of those games and *hope* that someone called us with the final scores so we could report them (often, nobody did). We were fortunate to have a satellite "feed" that gave us highlights of the professional games. But this feed didn't start until around 10:50 p.m. or so, and with the sportscast starting around 11:20 p.m., it made for some dicey moments before going on air. Long story short, in small market television, actually being on TV was often easier than the process it took to get there.

One perk of being an on-air "personality" in Binghamton in the late 1980s...I got tremendous exposure. Ours was the dominant station in town. Seemingly everyone watched our newscasts, so I was recognized a lot. It always makes me laugh when actors complain about having to interact or mingle with their fans. Why, then, do you act? Being recognized and talking to strangers is part of the gig, and most of us enjoy it, even if we don't freely admit it. To be 22 years old, just starting out in the "business," and getting recognized was really cool. And I always tried to be gracious when it happened. Someone once advised me to be nice to everyone, because if you are a jerk to one person, that person tells another person, and on it goes until word spreads that you are not friendly or approachable. And—like an actor—it doesn't take long for a TV news personality to garner a negative reputation if he or she doesn't treat people well.

Another aspect of life as a TV personality involved representing my station at local events. One time I had the opportunity to play with the Washington Generals against the Harlem Globetrotters. As you might expect, the Globetrotters had a field day messing around with me on the court. My worst moment was when I got fouled and was sent to the foul line for two free throws. There was a large crowd at Broome County Arena and I was nervous, so nervous I airballed both free throws, a total embarrassment for someone who had a decent high school career as a point guard at Palo Alto High School where I played with Jim Harbaugh (yes, that Jim Harbaugh), who led us to the sectional title game during his senior season.

But my overriding thought while in Binghamton was "I have to move on as quickly as possible." It was for me a 24/7 near compulsion. Sometimes it felt like a panic. Everything I did was motivated by moving to the next step, getting the next job. I could not shake the horrifying question, *"What if I got stuck here?"* It is a relentless, infuriating process to find the next opportunity because no one is going to come looking for you (much less find you) in a small market. My station recorded every newscast, and anytime I thought I did something worthy, I made sure to save the video. Problem was, these "aircheck" tapes were old and reused countless times, so the recordings often had defects (or weren't started on time), which led to potentially good material not being usable.

And there was another significant problem. The lighting in Binghamton was not good, and I looked terrible on the set, to the point that any resume tape I put together was really not presentable because I always looked like I had dark bags under my eyes. People frequently mentioned how tired I looked, which would in turn trigger the "I am never gonna get the next job" paranoia.

Thankfully, I had developed a relationship with a former Binghamton sportscaster who was working in Harrisburg, PA. There was an opportunity to fill in on the weekends at his station, and I did this as often as I could. That meant leaving my "main" job at 11:30 p.m., hopping in my grandma's Chevy Caprice (which had seen better days), and trekking three hours down Interstate 81 to Harrisburg in the middle of the night. Scary. Dark and late and lonely and lots of trucks. There was always construction. I drove through the hills of Pennsylvania, arriving in Harrisburg at 2:30 a.m. so I could put in 14-hour work days on Saturday and Sunday, all because I needed better-looking material for my resume tape in order to get out of Binghamton!

One Monday morning on the return trip, I had to navigate a terrible snowstorm. Five miles an hour, barely able to see, back through the hills of Pennsylvania up I-81, battling the trucks, just to get back to work on time. Dangerous. I should not have been on the road. What if I got stuck? What if I didn't make it back? I couldn't call in sick because my roommates were also my work colleagues and they knew I had been working in Harrisburg. I will never forget the snow finally stopping as I hit Scranton, enabling me to drive the final 60 miles stress-free for an on-time arrival at work. Again, all of this just to make my resume tape look more presentable. I look back on it, and I'm almost embarrassed by my ambition. It was all-consuming.

About six months after I arrived in Binghamton, the lead sportscaster, who spent years trying to get out of the market, finally did so, getting a job in Louisiana. I got promoted to the main sports job, bumping my salary to a whopping $15,000 a year. Karl Ravech, with whom I worked in Ithaca, was hired as our weekend sportscaster. And Trey Wingo worked at the ABC affiliate in town. So much talent in this one tiny market. We all subscribed to *MediaLine*, a nightly recording of job listings around the country. We all sent out resume tapes to every corner of the country. I was such a frequent visitor to the post office that the people working there would ask me, "Where is the tape going today, Bill?"

But what choice did we have if we wanted to take the next step? 999 times out of 1,000, the tapes and cover letters went out with no response. Karl used to joke it was like hitting golf balls into the water. The tapes would go out, and they would never come back.

The competition among local stations was also fierce. There was another young sportscaster at the local NBC affiliate who broke the story of former Yankees manager Billy Martin's death in the nearby town of Fenton. My general manager called me into his office to rip me for not having the story. Another time, Binghamton native Mayumi Pejo was arriving at the Syracuse airport after winning her bronze medal in the 1988 Summer Olympics in taekwondo at the age of 16. She landed at 5:00 p.m. All the newscasts ended at 6:30 p.m. Who was going to win the 70-mile race down I-81 from Syracuse to Binghamton to get the Pejo interview on the air before the newscasts ended? The guy from NBC got it on. My photographer and I didn't make it back to our station in time.

About a year after my promotion, I signed with a young agent in a big talent agency. I thought I had it made. Little did I know that those agencies sign countless clients, and have this annoying habit of sending multiple clients' tapes to the same job openings. That was an important lesson to learn. The agency (or agent) only cares about its bottom line, which entails making money from *any one* of its clients, conflict of interest be darned.

In the summer of 1989, after two years and countless trips to the post office and countless rejections and/or non-responses from stations, I was offered the weekend job at the NBC affiliate in Syracuse for $22k a year. Why then? Why that station? These are things that can never be explained. I told my agent about my first interview, and when I went up for a second interview, the news director showed me that my agent had submitted five other candidates for the job AFTER I had told him about the initial interview. The agent's response: "I had an obligation to all my clients who were interested in the opening."

I spent six months in Syracuse (where Mike Tirico was the lead sportscaster at the CBS affiliate). Then it was on to the Mizzou Sports News Network—which went out of business ten months later—and after that, unemployment. A freelance stint as a field producer at *Scholastic Sports America* at ESPN was next, and following a failed radio audition for the launch of ESPN Radio, I wound up in Boston as a sportscaster at New England Cable News (NECN). After a year and a half there, in February, 1993, my new agent (also Keith Olbermann's agent at the time) got me an audition for a spot on *SportsCenter*. I ended up auditioning in a group that included Ravech, who got the job! It all worked out, though, as six months later I was hired for the launch of ESPN2. Wingo followed me to ESPN in 1996.

It hasn't been easy. None of it. After 15 years at ESPN, I found myself again unemployed—and even got my license to sell life insurance—when I became an original hire on the Mad Dog Radio Network on Sirius XM. A year later, in September, 2009, I joined MSG Network in New York.

Here's the moral of my story—or pretty much anyone's in this line of work—as offered to me by Dennis Denninger, who hired me to work as a field producer on the aforementioned ESPN *Scholastic Sports America* and is now a professor at Syracuse: "As hard as it may be at times, you have to hold on to the surfboard. Never let it go. Because you never know when your wave might come.

"The Path Less Traveled"

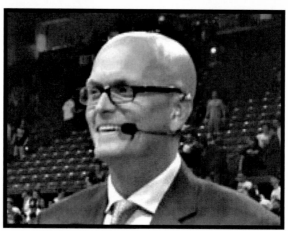

-From The Author:

  There were a thousand questions I had to address in putting this book together, but one thing I knew from the jump: Scott Van Pelt would be the final chapter. Not because he's the superstar that he is, but because his story is the anti-story. The George Costanza, if you will. The opposite of every "normal" journey into the upper echelon of sports TV. SVP is the exception that proves the rule, at least according to the rule book of 20 years ago—which is, admittedly, becoming outdated. I remember hosting an ESPNews *show with Scott shortly after he was hired, having heard through the grapevine that he was on the fast track to* SportsCenter *and would inevitably "leapfrog" many of us in the anchor pecking order within weeks. I'll be honest, I didn't get it at first. Which is why I am not (and never will be) a TV executive. He was raw, very much an unfinished product. And now I know why. I also know he is among the most talented sportscasters on the planet. Please understand, what SVP does on a nightly basis is the absolute highest level of television broadcasting. Degree of difficulty: off the charts. Seamlessly hosting a highlight-interview-analysis-opinion-banter show and excelling in every aspect, all the while making the viewer feel 1,000% comfortable. It is truly a gift. So rather than question the crazy confluence of factors that brought him into the national spotlight, I choose to simply appreciate that it actually happened.*

Scott Van Pelt

·North American Mortgage   ·ESPN
·The Golf Channel   ·ESPN Radio

Kearney, Nebraska.

If my chapter were going to follow the market-to-market script that many others have, it might have started there. I was interning at Fox Channel 5 in Washington, D.C., for Steve Buckhantz. As we were batting around the idea of the "Thin Man," as Buck called me, attempting to start an on-air journey, Kearney was the market that had an opening. I'd like to take this opportunity to say to the fine people of Kearney, the state of Nebraska, and that entire region of the country—I mean no offense with what I'm about to say next: There was no way on earth I was going to Kearney.

It had nothing to do with the place; it had everything to do with me. I heard a tremendous sound bite recently from Pittsburgh Steelers head coach Mike Tomlin. He's my favorite orator among head coaches. His way with the language, his command of it, I find amazing. He said, "It's not what you're capable of, it's what you're willing to do. I know plenty of people who are capable, I know fewer that are willing." I have no idea if I was capable of going there and learning the trade, but I *know* I wasn't willing to leave the D.C. area where I'd been my whole life, to move to Kearney just after I'd experienced the loss of my dad. Even had THEY been willing to have ME, which is assuming a lot, I'd never have made it. I didn't have it in my belly to make that sacrifice at that time. Had I tried, you'd never have known my name.

Thankfully, there was another guy at Channel 5 at the time who is the reason you do. Paul Farnsworth was Buck's producer. I showed up in a suit for my intern interview; he looked at me, flummoxed. "If you can fog a mirror, you are qualified to be an intern. You don't need to wear a suit." There was more to it than that, but Farns had an amazing way of putting people at ease. His smile, his laugh, and his attitude were infectious and even if you didn't know it, or if he wasn't doing it willfully, he was teaching. He was a great audience and always made me feel like he was my biggest fan. That would be huge a couple years later.

During those years post-internship, let's just be charitable and say your boy did not thrive. I had a number of jobs. Most involved selling things. "With your personality, you could sell anything." Let's re-visit that Tomlin quote—I wasn't *willing*. I didn't want to hassle people I knew to buy stocks or insurance. I damn sure didn't want to try to sell stuff to people I didn't know. Cold calling, sales role-play? No thanks. Man, I sold beepers (a misnomer as I don't think I actually *sold* any to anyone. I did some equipment swaps, though!). I peddled mortgages. (The only thing I was truly elite at for North American Mortgage was the Jumble. I will kick your a$$ at the Jumble. We had this Burger King crown we got and wrote the name of the Jumble winner on the inside of it. My name was all over that thing.) I was not, however, generating a ton of new business and...I got fired the week before Christmas. Deserved it.

I was getting ready to take a job with an insurance and securities firm. White shirts, ties...grown up stuff. But somewhere in that time frame, I got a call from Farns. He had been in New York working with HBO and MSG and they were getting ready to start something called The Golf Channel. "VP, you gotta come down here and work for me, what are you even doing up there right now?" Getting unemployment and destroying my credit, that's what I thought in my head.

There was this joint in Bethesda, Maryland, on Wisconsin Avenue at the time—it was 1994—called T Bones. It was the spot. Post-college bar, Monday burger night, you get the drill. I was eating lunch there one afternoon with a buddy named Mick Carbury. I lived in Mick's house at the time and we were talking about The Golf Channel and I was telling him I wasn't sure I wanted to go...didn't know what it was going to be...blah, blah, blah. Mick told me, point blank, "You have to go. You have nothing going here, and eventually it's going to get bad. You've got to start over. Re-invent yourself." Mick and I weren't like close friends; he was just the unlucky guy whose house I was crashing in at the time. But he was 1,000% right. I had to go. I owed Mick about three months' rent for years. I sent him a check not long ago. He's done very well for himself, and said I didn't have to do it. I explained I needed to square it cosmically with the universe. We're even. But not really. Without his nudge, who knows if I'd have packed up a Ryder truck to go to Orlando.

At The Golf Channel (TGC), I was a PA: Production Associate. I've seen the story told repeatedly that I worked in the tape library. That's simply not accurate. Now, I spent a good amount of time down there playing "H-O-R-S-E." Shout to my man Aaron Deboni and Drake Schunk. D-bone won the showcase on *The Price is Right*, by the way. Just thought I'd share that tidbit. But I was not in the library, thank you very much—I was a PA. What did I do? I'm sure a lot of people there asked themselves that question often. I cut down some *Shell's Wonderful World of Golf* shows to make them fit into an hour or half-hour window. If you want to know about Chi Chi Rodriguez at Dorado Beach, I'm your guy. All of us were trying to figure out what the hell we were going to do to fill 24 hours a day with just golf. Keep in mind, we didn't have the kind of rights they have now. Had you told any of us in the fall of '94 that someday the US Open and the Open championship would be on The Golf Channel, along with the PGA tour, we'd have all laughed hysterically. We were just trying to fill hours and days with whatever. Anything. Literally.

One of the pillars of the primetime lineup was going to be *Golf Talk Live*. The host was Peter Kessler. One day, I think it was November, maybe December, of '94, Farns told me to be in the studio at 3:00 p.m. "For what?" I asked. He was vague …something about rehearsal. Whatever. I show up at three and they tell me that I'm going to be Arnold Palmer.

Mr. Palmer (which was what I always called him, even after we knew each other) was an investor with the channel and was going to be the first big guest, and this was just a rehearsal for the director and camera crew, as well as Peter, to just sort out the feel of the show. So, I'm in there all loosey-goosey having some fun answering questions like I'm actually Arnold Palmer. Which beats the heck out of role-playing beeper sales. I'm the king, baby!

So the story goes that in the control room, Mike Whelan, the executive VP of The Golf Channel, is standing there with his index finger up against his lip looking at the screen when he says, to nobody in particular, "Who is this?"

After a pause, someone answers, "What? That's Peter Kessler, your host. What are you even talking about?"

"No," he said, "Who is this idiot who thinks he's Arnold Palmer?"

See, my guy Farns was scheming all along. He remembered the dope in the suit who interned for him, and always thought I had something. What, exactly? Who knows? But...something. He wanted me in there that day to do exactly what I did. Get the attention of the guy who mattered there. Whelan.

From there, I did a few behind the scenes things—doing Peter Alliss accents over a golf tournament between TGC and *Golfweek*, where I did some interviews after the round. It was actually practice for the cameramen to shoot golf, which is an incredible skill you don't just *have*. So the event served a purpose for them. For me, once again, it was a chance to show that I had...something. None of it mattered. It wasn't actually on air. But remember what I said about TGC as it launched: we were simply filling time. And not long after we launched in January of '95, they actually had me go do a "package" (feature story) for *Golf Central*. It was a charity event hosted by Chi Chi, my guy from Dorado Beach. It got rained out, but I still interviewed a bunch of big-name players, including Jack Nicklaus. It was that day I learned that standing too close to the people I was interviewing was a no-no. I'm 6'6", and you could look right up Jack's nose as he looked up at me.

Anyway, I did a predictably bad standup about the rain "doing little to dampen the spirits," we cut a package and it aired on TV. We got word that the boss, Joe Gibbs—not football/NASCAR Joe Gibbs, but Alabama businessman Joe

Gibbs—wasn't thrilled that some PA was on TV. But at the time, we weren't on as many TVs as there are in Kearney, Nebraska, so it wasn't like I was setting the network backward. Thankfully, they let me keep doing packages for shows. Then they let me host a show called the *Leaderboard Report*. Looking back, it was awesome practice, because even though it was taped, it was a 15-minute segment in one straight shot. Editing has come a long way since then. But the way we were doing it, you couldn't bust out of a segment. You either had to fight through a screwup, or stop and start over. That led to some long tapings for a 15-minute show. Because I was a complete rookie, I had zero training in this. I hadn't done any TV anywhere in my life. But here I was doing it.

The concept of the show now sounds just brutal—a scroll of the scores from the PGA, LPGA, and Senior tours with minimal highlights and me adding some snippet about birdies/bogies, what have you. Sign me up for some of that! But again, it was tremendous practice and I was grateful. I had a show. Are you kidding me?

That was where learning how to anchor a broadcast began. Where I began to grow comfortable with the process, which is the most important thing you can be as a host. If you're comfortable, you put your viewer at ease. When I sat down with David Feherty as the guest on his brilliant show, I don't know that I felt particularly comfortable (which was evident watching those pieces back), but it's all part of the journey—and I'm proud of all it, as unlikely as it is.

The trajectories of my journey and my then-employer's were both changed by the same guy—Tiger Woods. He truly burst onto the scene as TGC was launching and I was getting opportunities in front of the camera. In May of 1995, I was sent to cover the NCAA championships from the Scarlet Course in Columbus, Ohio. I've often said it, because it's the truth: I was no more a reporter than I was an astronaut. Which is to say, I had no formal training in either. But there I was, reporting on this event. It was actually an incredible tournament. Oklahoma State beat Stanford—and their freshman phenom—in a playoff. Throughout that week, after I met Tiger, we began to get to know each other. At the time, as a twenty-something who really didn't know what the heck he was doing, I guess I seemed more approachable than others in the media. Maybe I'm flattering myself. Whatever the case, Tiger and I began developing a professional relationship, if for no other reason than I kept turning up at events where he was playing—and winning: the '96 NCAA Championship in Tennessee, the '96 Amateur in Pumpkin Ridge in Oregon, then the '97 Masters.

Following that win, TGC was hoping we could get some time with him for a segment in advance of the '98 Masters. I drove three and a half hours from Orlando to Miami and waited to speak with Tiger in the locker room at Doral. It was just me sitting there when he walked in. I asked if we could talk the week of Bay Hill (prior to The Masters). He said sure. "Did you really drive all the way down here just to ask me this?" I can't remember if I lied at the time, but that's why I'd driven there.

The day I was supposed to speak with Tiger, I ran into Jimmy Roberts, then with ESPN. "You here to talk to Tiger, too?" he asked.

"I don't know about 'too'," I responded, "but I am here to talk to Tiger."

He said, "I'll flip you to see who goes first." I don't know why I was so bold. Jimmy was, and is, a friend. But I explained that I had driven to Miami weeks earlier to set this up and I wasn't flipping anybody for anything. I was going first.

Good thing.

I was told I had five minutes. When I sat down, I had a yellow legal pad in my lap. I knew every shot he'd hit, knew the quotes, knew it all. What I did not know was that Tiger Woods had never really done what we were about to do, which was such a massive win for me. Because when we started, he was suddenly back at Augusta in '97, it was Thursday, the start of one of most memorable Masters tournaments in history, and he was about to take us along for the walk. Through the thoughts and the emotions, all the way into Earl's arms on Sunday. It was riveting. It was also about 45 minutes. His agents wanted to kill me. But Tiger didn't. Whether he'd intended to or not, giving me what he did, the way he did, put me on the map. Because nobody else got that. By the time he got to Jimmy, he was out of ammo. Sorry about that, my guy.

I got back to TGC and went into the office of a senior producer named Jeff Hymes. "Scotty, we got a segment?" I said, nope. His face fell.

"We got a f***ing *show*." I took him to the back into an edit bay and put the tape in. Nobody said anything for a long, long time. Some bigwigs made their way down and were watching in amazement from the hall.

At some point, Jeff grabbed my neck and said, "Scotty, we got a f***ing show."

As everyone knows, Tiger went on to do outrageous things on golf courses in the coming years, and if we fast-forward the tape to 2000, Jimmy Roberts, my fellow Maryland grad and friend, re-enters the picture. He leaves ESPN for NBC in the midst of Tiger winning every major he plays in. He's the biggest name and story in sports, and ESPN's golf reporter leaves, creating a massive opening. On my desk I have a Post-it note which reads: "I will never work at ESPN." I signed it on 4/30/96. That was the day a TGC producer named Lee "Nate" Rosenblatt, who was a former ESPN-er, insisted I was going to end up there. I said I wouldn't. I signed the Post-it note as part of a hundred-dollar bet.

So I lost 100 bucks.

The funny thing is, if TGC would simply have offered me a LITTLE more money, I probably wouldn't have lost the $100. Remember the conversation back at T-Bones with Mick? I am a creature of habit. And as opposed to *having* to leave DC, I didn't *have* to leave here. I really loved the place and what I did. I was comfortable. I was happy. I didn't need to be at ESPN to feel like I'd made it. Remember, mine is the chapter that makes no sense. I didn't have a path or a goal; it was all just sort of happening. So when ESPN came to me with an offer, I expected TGC to offer that PLUS something. Even a dollar, right? I will leave out the part about how they kept paying me like a PA even after I was on TV for a while, because it all worked out just fine. But when the time came for TGC to step up and offer "x + $1," what they came with was actually "x - $1." Now, I'm not the smartest guy in the world, but that didn't make any sense at all to me. To be fair, I didn't have an agent then. I took all of it personally, which is a common mistake. It's always business, never personal (that's Nino Brown). I explained I had to think about some things and we left it that way as I was heading on the road for an event.

Me being me, I was still trying to figure out a way to stay. To *not* try the "new thing." But that's when, to quote Jules from *Pulp Fiction*, "I had what alcoholics refer to as a moment of clarity." I was sitting outside at an In-N-Out in Vegas with my cameraman Big Al, and Fred Couples. If I ever write the book about the road with Big Al, I'll need to change some names to protect the guilty. Anyway, it was just as plain as day—what am I doing? ESPN is offering me this chance, am I an idiot? Rhetorical. Don't answer that. I picked up the phone and called The Golf Channel and told them I was going to accept ESPN's offer.

They tried to get me to change my mind, which was kind of them, but I knew the opportunity was too much to pass up. I had no clue that 20+ years later I'd be as fortunate as I've been. But, it's clear that at least one time outside an In-N-Out in Vegas someone made a decision that actually made sense.

It's been a joy to jot this down. I've been texting with my man Big Al, remembering it all, and thankful for where it led. I realize what I always do: this path isn't repeatable. Not that I am so unique. But my circumstances undoubtedly are. Unless you just happen to have an "in" with someone who can get you a gig at a niche network about to launch, where you will get an on-air opportunity with zero experience, then meet and develop an excellent working relationship with the single biggest sports star on planet Earth. I mean…just do that, right?

I suppose I am proof that anything is possible in this goofy business. I wasn't willing to go to Kearney. Thankfully, I showed I was capable in Orlando. A little more than a decade ago, it all came full circle. We were shooting a "*This Is SportsCenter*" ad in the cafeteria. It was me, Stuart Scott and Arnold Palmer. The concept was simple: Arnold Palmer *makes* an Arnold Palmer. Little lemonade, little tea, he walks off. Stuart and I mumble to each other under our breath, "That was awesome."

I wonder if he ever knew that the whole thing started because I walked into a studio one afternoon and pretended I was him.

If you shake your head as this chapter concludes at just how improbable the whole thing is, I assure you I did the same as I wrote it.

"So, Now What?"

Improbable.

SVP's final descriptor couldn't be more accurate. I mean, a fired mortgage broker moves to Florida on a whim and winds up becoming one of the most popular sports broadcasters on the planet? Seriously?

Of course, as you now realize, *every* success story in this book is improbable. It's simply a matter of degree.

I noted earlier that Chris Berman got lucky by being in the right place at the right time. Truth is, we all did. Luck, like talent, is a prerequisite for TV sports success. It's a numbers game, and the numbers are not favorable.

Funny thing is, it's those long odds that spawned the stories in this book. If it were easy to reach the major leagues, Dave Flemming would not have had to wash jock straps. If it were easy to reach ESPN, Jaymee Sire would not have had to lug 40 pounds of camera equipment on her 100-pound frame. We are the sum of our experiences, and the very nature of the business has made those experiences so extraordinary.

Twenty years from now, this book would look quite different. The rules are changing. Just as ESPN and subsequent sports networks re-shaped the TV landscape in the late 20th century, the proliferation of digital and streaming options is doing the same today. And with the evolution (devolution?) of the industry, the hiring process has shifted dramatically. Writing ability and broadcast experience have been devalued relative to internet "popularity." The age of the influencer is upon us.

Not coincidentally, TV news departments continue to marginalize sports at an alarming rate. Many stations have downsized sports departments or, in some cases, eliminated them altogether. Yet demand for sports jobs remains through the roof. I slept through much of Economics 101 in college, but I do understand why salaries are therefore plummeting. While bottom-barrel wages have long been the norm in small-market TV, the disturbing reality is most large-market jobs pay a fraction of what they did a decade ago. TV sports anchors are still celebrities, but most are no longer paid like them.

The future of the industry is, in Kenny Mayne's words, a story for a different book. My goal was to embrace the past, which I could not have done without the help of my friends. So thank you, Lindsey, for planting the seed; thank you, Paul, for believing in the concept; thank you, Jen, for giving me the time and space to write (and re-write); and most of all, thank you contributors for allowing me to share your journeys.

In the words of the great Bill Pidto, "It's been a good run, Shug." I'd be lying if I said I wouldn't change a thing, but I can say without a shred of doubt, the end has more than justified the means.

About The Author

Scott Reiss is an Emmy Award-winning sports broadcaster who has spent the last quarter-century living the TV dream, while honing his craft at the local, regional, and national levels of television.

Scott's journey began at Beverly Hills High School, where he stumbled upon a broadcast journalism class during his senior year. He became the sports anchor on a class-produced weekly news broadcast that aired on local cable access TV, and he was hooked.

Scott later graduated with honors from Stanford University, having earned a bachelor's degree in communication and a master's degree in sociology. After a year of job hunting and soul searching, he moved 2,200 miles east to begin his TV career in Panama City, Florida. That career path led him through Utica, New York and Santa Maria, California before his "big break" at age 29, when he was hired as an anchor at ESPN.

During his eight years in Bristol, Scott hosted pretty much every show on the network, including *SportsCenter*, *Baseball Tonight*, *NFL Live*, and *College Gamenight*. He also hosted ESPN Radio's *College Gameday*, which taught him that if you can execute seven straight hours of live radio on a college football Saturday, you can handle pretty much anything in the broadcasting world.

The ESPN experience was as educational as it was humbling, as it allowed Scott to learn from the best TV professionals in the business—both in front of and behind the camera. It also put him in position to make another "dream" come true, returning home to California to work in major-market television.

In 2008, Scott was hired as the lead anchor for the Comcast SportsNet Bay Area startup in San Francisco. The timing couldn't have been better, as he was tasked with hosting pregame and postgame shows for the Giants as they won three World Series in five years. Some of his greatest professional memories stem from those shows, both in San Francisco and in the various American League cities.

After five years at CSN, Scott was offered still another "dream" opportunity: to become the radio play-by-play voice of his alma mater. He has been calling Stanford football and basketball games since 2013, while spending much of that time also working as a sports anchor/reporter at KTVU, the FOX affiliate in the Bay Area.

Scott currently lives in Walnut Creek, California, with his beautiful wife, Jennifer, and their two wonderful boys, Lucas and Cody.

Made in United States
North Haven, CT
06 December 2022